Rwanda

Ye

Rwanda Yesterday

PATRICIA
BAMURANGIRWA

Matador
9 Priory Business Park
Kibworth Beauchamp
Leicestershire LE8 0RX, UK
Tel: (+44) 116 279 2299
Fax: (+44) 116 279 2277
Email: books@troubador.co.uk
Web: www.troubador.co.uk/matador

ISBN 978 1783060 412

British Library Cataloguing in Publication Data.
A catalogue record for this book is available from the British Library.

Printed and bound in the UK by TJ International, Padstow, Cornwall
Typeset in 11pt Bembo by Troubador Publishing Ltd, Leicester, UK

Matador is an imprint of Troubador Publishing Ltd

BRIEF AUTOBIOGRAPHY OF THE AUTHOR PATRICIA SINZI BAMURANGIRWA

I was born in 1948, the last born out of six: three girls and three boys to my parents Tarcice Rutabagisha Sinzi and Bagerobeza, in a town called Butare in Rwanda.

I was in primary school in 1960, when the war broke out in various parts of Rwanda and that was the end of my education.

In 1961, Mathias Misago, who had recently taken over the leadership of our town, demolished our homestead because he did not get along with my father. The main war hadn't spread to that area yet but we became the first family to flee in the village, leaving our relatives, friends and all that we owned.

We first escaped to Congo in 1963, when the war of Mulele broke out and spread quickly all over the country: we did not have any other choice than to seek refugee in Uganda. After some time, my father wanted to be independent, to not depend on his children, to be somewhere he could be himself and start again and to become a farmer as before. As far as he was concerned, living without cows was to miss something important in his life. That is why he chose to go to the neighbouring country of Tanzania. In the middle of this drama, I missed and lost the opportunity to pursue my education, which was my main lifelong ambition.

In 1971, I moved to Nairobi (Kenya) as I wanted to start life on my own. I found a partner and gave birth to my son, Manzi Sinzi Emmanuel. Unfortunately, my relationship with his father did not last for long and we separated.

I started another relationship, and gave birth to my daughter, Niwegaju Greiner Sinzi. I didn't want any more intimate relationships, as I feared I would go through the same bad experiences I had had in the past.

I chose to take care of my sister's children, as well as my own and raised seven children in total. I tried my best to prove to them that I was able and I gave them the opportunities that I did not get. Through the will of God, I am proud that each one of them has grown up to be a respectable and well-rounded individual in every way.

On the other hand, I tried to educate myself in every way possible. I had the ambition of knowing the reason behind the conflicts in the world and if there were any solutions at all. I wanted to find out why most of the leaders of the world were not happy to fight for peace and these thoughts led me to carry on research from people of all kinds of backgrounds: people on the street, the educated, the older generation, politicians and those who were in the Rwandan monarchy, such as Rwandan King Ndahindurwa V and his family. This is how I got the idea of putting my findings into writing, so that the truth can be there for everyone to read and I really hope that this book will help those willing to know.

PREFACE

RATIONALE

This book is an overview of the political situation of the country that has brought the involvement of many other countries in regional affairs. It is quite obvious that this new aspect of history is not at all unique. Many authors have been writing extensively about Rwanda, with both positive and negative views on Rwandan society and how it has been advanced.

This summary, however shallow and brief, attempts to put clarity to the real course of history and to expel anomalies that have become a source of confusion among many Rwandans. What makes my book special is not narrating events of Rwanda's history, but to seek to provide some clarity on the cause rather than the effects of the current state of affairs. It divides the history into its evolutionary epochs and highlights the characteristics of each epoch.

The first epoch dismisses the misconception that the history of Rwanda started with the movement of its people from the Middle East. It disentangles a Munyarwanda from the erroneous historical preposition that Rwanda was, and is, inhabited by three different races. Such is the view of many Western people, among them Gil Courtemanche who says that:

> "The Tutsi who had reigned over Ruanda-Urundi for centuries, had come from the North, from Egypt or Ethiopia. Hamitic people were not true Negroes but were probably whites darkened by centuries of sun. Their tall stature, the paleness of their skin and the fineness of their features attested to this noble ancestry." (Courtemanche: 2003, 23).

vii

The epoch shows how a Munyarwanda began his existing history, when he first freed himself from the fetters of nature, and started his historical journey, which lasted hundreds of thousands of years, until this historical evolution was invaded and negated by colonization.

The purpose of this historical summary is obvious: visionary Rwandans do not engage in writing history just for pleasure. The principal task of such an attempt is to put clarity on the real course of history. It is therefore important to understand Rwanda's successive epochs of history, in order to understand today's nature and character of the contradiction. The Chinese say that: "the past had to teach the present".

Because of the size of this book, I have found it necessary to look at every stage of history, in the introduction, so that a true picture of the process is seen before perusing into the book. We cannot, however, claim that a book of this form projects the social fabrics of the Rwandan society, but an attempt has been made to give an insight into the core of our problems.

Rwanda had been turned into a playground. Overlooking this may be considered as a failure to do good service to the people of Rwanda, and more particularly to the youth, who are yet to know the source of the country's sorry state of affairs. Some Rwandans may disagree but this summary is a positive glimpse at the real course of history.

This glimpse of the history of Rwanda owes its birth from discussion and debates with my Rwandan friends, who have been taking an active interest in what has been going on in Rwanda, in particular, and in the region known as the "Great Lakes".

What has been taking place in Rwanda, has been a response to the demands, set forth by the neo-colonial conditions, imposed on the country since Africa's emergency into the political arena in the 1960s, after testing bitter pills of colonial dependency domination.

I feel that this book will appeal to people with first-hand experience of the evolution of the Rwandan society. The epochs give an overview of the progressive growth, development, and later, retrogression of the history of Rwandan growth and development because, by the time of the invitation to Rwanda by colonialists, Rwanda had emerged from a large community of Kinyarwanda speaking people. They occupied the largest part, which is now known as the Great Lakes region of Africa, extending from today's Rwanda and Burundi, to the Western part of Uganda, Eastern Congo and Western Tanzania. It was an organised society under a large kingdom and retrogression because when colonialism set foot on the soil of Rwanda, its state formation was completely destroyed by colonialism. I have divided this summary of Rwandan history into the following phases.

THE COLONIAL EPOCH

Writers of the history of Rwanda say that, the first explorers were struck by social division between the Tutsi, Hutu and Twa groups. Many authors, among them Prunier, have been talking of Bahutu, as a typical Bantu race, originating from either the South or Central Africa or from the Central Region. Their historical view was distorted, as John Hanning Speke stated: "Tutsi were superior to the Hutu." He wrote that, "the rulers of the various kingdoms in the Great Lakes region of Africa must have come from a conquering race, and brought a superior civilization" (Guillebaud: 2002, 34).

Tutsi originates from the Galla region of Ethiopia or from Egypt or Asia Minor. They have described Batwa as the "Aboriginals of Rwanda", with a face like a monkey and huge noses, with similarities to apes. In saying this, they were only guessing because there are no facts at all.

Therefore, the author dismisses this proposition, and gives lighter note of the real origin of a Munyarwanda. The book gives a brief view of a Munyarwanda, as a product of an evolution until his journey was barred by colonial invasion and domination. The processes of Rwanda's growth and development stopped following the invasion of the country by German colonialists from 1885-1919. Later, Rwanda jumped from Germany's frying pan to the Belgian's fire, from 1916 to 1962.

This book asserts that colonialism has never been indirect. Indeed, some came out of curiosity, as it was the time of new discoveries. Others came just to propagate and to advance their church's doctrine among the people they thought were living in darkness. People such as David Livingstone or Stanley Morgan, just to name those few in Central Africa.

1

However, after getting to know Africa and realising that it is so rich, most of them changed their mission and began to sell their discoveries among Western countries. That is how the misery of many Africans started because the main focus became plundering resources; it marked the end of Rwanda's independence and ushered in an epoch of dependency. This peep at the colonial era is a reminder of how colonialism destroyed the power of the kingdom and how its economic gain necessitated political and cultural domination and dependency. The divide and rule policy of colonialists that changed Rwanda's production castes to be tribes or races, has been criticized in this book. It shows the aim of the policy as a means, compiling the races in order to create neo-colonial hangers-on.

The principal contradiction, between colonialists and their church on the one hand and the *umwami* (the king) and his chiefs on the other, is a basic understanding of the cause of genocide in Rwanda, both in the colonial and neo-colonial times. The contradiction culminated into open confrontation between colonialists and Banyarwanda leaders. It is historian, Gerald Prunier who spoke about the root of the Rwandan problem: "It is essential to keep this process in mind in order to understand the transformation which took place in Rwanda between 1860 and 1931 and which directly gave birth to its modern society - and its almost intractable problems" (Prunier: 1995,21).

Meg Guillebaud adds to this concept: "The theory had an impact on the Rwandans themselves since the Tutsi began to see themselves as "born to rule" even if they were thoroughly disadvantaged, and the Hutu developed a massive inferiority complex which made them very resentful of even the poorest Tutsi". (Guillebaud: 2002,34).

In Africa, the 1950s and 1960s are of historical importance. They remind Africans about their struggle for self-determination. Progressive political analysts say that, when colonialism is faced with an imperative crisis, it massacres whatever it can get hold of. In his book, *The Wretched of the Earth*, Frantz Fanon says that: "the last battle of the colonized against the colonizer, will, often, be the fight of the colonized against each other".

2

The same book discusses what colonial Belgium called the 1959 revolution. The extermination of Batutsi by the colonizers, through and with the colonized, proved that Fanon's observation was verified in Rwanda, during the struggle for independence.

Some old people saw Rwanda's genocide as the most systematic human massacre ever witnessed since the extermination of the Jews by Hitler. After that extermination, a flag of independence was granted to Rwanda as UNOS' resolution. However, the question was not independence, but who got it.

THE NEO-COLONIAL EPOCH

The book is a reminder of how Parmehutu was a creation of the colonial authority through the Catholic Church, and how independence was imposed upon Parmehutu, in spite of opposing it. They had vehemently rejected the idea, and preferred what they termed "equality with the Batutsi".

In July 1962, a puppet regime of Kayibanda and his Parmehutu was installed in Kigali, to supervise the Belgian fief. The book shows how nationalists, with their supporters, were condemned to perpetual exit by the regime and its mentors. It also shows how and why a change of the guards took place in 1973, when Kayibanda was overthrown by his army chief, Habyarimana. General Habyarimana's regime was not different from that of his predecessor, Kayibanda, the author reveals. Indeed the comrade role of Habyarimana was deeper than Kayibanda's. This book gives a brief glimpse of the regime.

THE REVOLUTION IN RWANDA

In 1987, the Rwandan Patriotic Front emerged from an alliance that was formed as early as 1979 by Rwanda's refugees. This book traced the original of the Rwanda alliance for national unity and the formation of the R.P.F as a liberation front. The front organised different movements outside and inside Rwanda and started a civil war in 1990. The front also launched a politic and diplomatic offensive, which later culminated into the signing of a power-sharing agreement with the regime in Kigali. As expected, Hayarimana's regime refused to abide by the accord and on the advice of the French government, planned the extermination of Batutsi, who were inside the country, in order to pre-empt R.P.F's strategy. This book is a good reference to remind us of Habyarimana's plan, with his collaborator Ntaryamira of Burundi, to regionalise the conflict and to call the war, a conflict of Batutsi against Bahutu in the whole region.

The plane carrying Habyarimana, Ntaryamira and their cohorts, was hit by two missiles just in the airport area. This book evaluated a number of reasons for Habyarimana's death. It also refutes the suggestion that his death was the cause of genocide.

THE SECOND GENOCIDE

The second genocide 1994, after the first one which happened in Rwanda 1959, soon after _Umwami_ (King) Mutara Rudahigwa's assissination

The ideology of extermination of Batutsi was a colonial strategy of pre-empting nationalism in Rwanda. This book traces the roots of the ideology from the Catholic Church in the 1920s, to the time of the struggle for independence by colonial agents, until it was concluded in 1994. The intervention of France to try to stop R.P.F is a clear testimony of the plan. This book does not only discuss the Rwanda genocide, it compares it with many other cases, where people were killed by tyrannical regimes. Many writers have extensively written about genocide in Rwanda. This book, however, considers genocide as an outcome of fascism and tyranny. The regime's _raison d'etre_ had entailed it was an obligation rather than a policy of hatred and cold-blooded revenge.

THE R.P.F CAPTURE OF POWER

The new government of National Unity was formed in Kigali on the 19ᵗʰ July 1994. A number of Rwandans, both in the country and in the Diaspora, are ignorant of the R.P.F. Some thought it was a group of exiled Tutsi, who were power-hungry and organised war against Habyarimana's regime. Others are of the view that R.P.F was a tool of N.R.M of Uganda, used for the purpose of expanding Museven's rule or ambition. Few among these Rwandans, who claim to have a political vision, say that R.P.F was a front of Rwandans both in and outside the country, uniting all forces that could be united in order to wage struggle, against an agent regime. This book concisely gives different views about the front by both Rwandans and non-Rwandans.

This book also highlights the role of the French government, in the political direction of the Habyarimana regime. There are many known cases where tyrannical regimes in Africa have been kept in power, by their mentors. Rwanda's case was not unique. After being defeated, Habyarimana's army, together with their French collaborators, took a population of about two million to Zaire. A view of this situation has been given in this book.

The French government and their Mobutu of Zaire, were determined to reorganise their genocidal army. Training camps were set up, and centres of recruitment established. This book identifies some of the prominent personalities that were involved in the strategic planning of Rwanda's invasion.

The camps of new refugees in Zaire were presenting a danger to the new government in Rwanda .The government, together with their supporters, were also making a plan to destroy those camps. This book comments on the destruction of the camps and on the consequences suffered by Mobutu's regime and his Habyarimana's army.

THE WAR OF LIBERATION IN ZAIRE

A discussion held by the author with a number of Congolese, as well as Rwandans, produced different views about the war in Zaire. This book brings those views to the reader in a summary form, but with emphasis on the essence of the war.

The Kabila factor is also brought to the notice of the reader because many Africans have been wondering how all the Congolese leaders, including Laurent Kabila, could abruptly jump to the helm of a liberation movement. In this book, the author is of the view that a pan-African strategy was first and foremost to get rid of Mobutu and then the issue of a visionary leadership later. As a negative force, Kabila had to struggle for political survival.

THE DEMOCRATIC REPUBLIC OF THE CONGO

For more than three decades Zaire had been a politico economic field of imperialism, with Mobutu viewed as one of the best boys on the continent. He was comparable to a few agents like Kamuzu Banda of Malawi, Haile Sellasie of Ethiopia and Jom Kenyata of Kenya.

Mobutu, in collusion with South African fascists, was instrumental to Savimbi's negative war against the people of the Republic of Angola. When the R. P. F waged liberation struggle against the agent's regime of Habyarimana, Mobutu sent 5,000 troops to the rescue of Habyarimana.

I have in this book tried to look at the alliance between the two agents, as a resistance against change.

Laurent Kabila, on the other hand, had been in exile for more than thirty years. He was a Lumumbist and, together with other MNC members, had waged unsuccessful struggle against Mobutu regimes. It is thought that Laurent Kabila was the only immediate Congolese to form the new unified government, in the absence of a revolutionary leader.

Pan-africanists had to take advantage of the objective developments in the country. I have suggested that the traitorous move, taken by Kabila against his creators, was not an accident of history, but was a result of opportunistic ambitions. He had no vision for the Congo, he had simply jumped on the bandwagon. After turning against his mentor, a new struggle by forces opposed to his leadership started with Zimbabwe, Angola and Namibia on his side, and Rwanda and Uganda on the other side of the rebels.

The decade of Laurent Kabila is referred in this book as a direct result of confrontation between the stakeholders in the politics of Congo. Political observers have given differing reasons of his death. This book brings to the reader's attention what people said about his death. This book also comments on what people said about the cause of the second war.

CONGO UNDER KABILA JUNIOR

After the assassination of Laurent Kabila, his son, Joseph, became Zimbabwe's choice. Sir Kweti Masire of Botswana had suffered a setback when Joseph Kabila was made Congolese President. Joseph was a product of Uganda, where he went to school and received basic military training. During his father's tenure of office he was made army chief through the pressure of the USA and European Union. Joseph Kabila accepted Masire's mediation. An agreement between parties involved in the conflict was reached in Lusaka. This book refers to some points of the agreements. There have been many agreements in Lusaka, Kampala and in South Africa, between the Kabila's government and rebels who were involved in the Congo conflict. At the time of compiling this book the most viable agreement was that of South Africa, about the withdrawal of troops of the countries involved and the formation of National Unity government. This book has briefly commented on the role of Rwanda in the Congo's equation and has forecast possible implications of the agreement on Rwanda's socio-political developments.

The Rwanda – Uganda clash in Congo has become an important phenomenon in Rwanda's history. Many people have been asking themselves the following:

•Was the confrontation between the two brotherly countries a war?

•Was it a mere confrontation as Uganda leaders called it?

•Was it a reflection of misunderstanding between commanders in Kisangani?

•Was it the product of a teacher – student relationship as leaders in Rwanda wanted us to believe?

•Was the confrontation caused by Clement who wanted to plunder Congo's natural resources as the European Union was propagating?

•Was it the result of Kagame's ideological bankruptcy, as claimed by Museveni in an open letter to Claire Short, who was the British Minister for overseas development at the time?

Political observers have failed to discover the main reason for that conflict. In this book we looked at the views from both countries. Analysts have also failed to discover the reason behind British mediation.

CONCLUSION

Finally, what is the purpose of a shallow history book of this form? It originates in response to many publications, especially recent erroneous books about Rwandan genocide. This book has been inspired by

Rwandans, who have an interest in the politics of their country. An attempt has been made to give an insight into the core of our problems. Rwanda has been turned into a playground. To overlook this may be considered a failure to do good service to the people of Rwanda and, more particularly, to the youth who are yet to know the source of the country's sorry state of affairs.

THE PRE – COLONIAL EPOCH

HUMAN OCCUPATION

The physical layout of Rwanda today cannot be of a historical reference because colonisation completely changed the country's pre-colonial setting. Some writers of books about Rwanda have justifiably asserted that Kinyarwanda-speaking people are found all over the Great Lakes region: Rwanda, Burundi, Western Uganda, Eastern Congo and Western Tanzania. The small portion of the region is what is known today as the Republic of Rwanda; it consists of 1,000 hills and covers an area of 26,338 km only.

Early authors of books about Rwanda, including Jean-Jacques Maquet, Mgr Leroy and many other European authors, have the same historical essence. The only early Munyarwanda writer was Mgr Alex Kagame, whose works are a popular reference to many writers. All these writers have proposed that the Rwandan society is divided into three groups: the Tutsi, Twa and Hutu. The groups, called tribes or races, are neither similar nor equal. It is said that early Europeans were smitten by the Tutsi race, and came to conclusion that the Tutsi were definitely too fine to be of Bantu origin. They also concluded that the Hutu group indicated that they were pure Negroes, displaying somatic characteristics.

All of these authors, including Rwandan writers like Kagame, have proposed that Batutsi are the Gara of Southern Ethiopia. Writing about the Bahima of Uganda, Sir John Hanaing talked of the conquest of an inferior race in the region. Bahima of the old Ankole kingdom are said to be Batutsi cousins. A number of writers go as far as talking about Hamitic origins of Batutsi and that they originated from a primordial red race.

Andrew Pages wrote a book to this effect. He called it: *Un Royaume Hamitic au Centre de l'Afrique*. Sir Harry Johnston wrote that kingships in the Interlacustrine region: the Great Lake region, originated from the Ethiopia empire and that they were pastoral invaders.

In 1920, Pierre Ryckmans, the then Belgian Governor, said that Batutsi were made to reign and that it was not surprising that the Bahutu had made themselves enslaved without goer or revolt. There were many theories, but what matters is that their objective, whether cautiously or not, is a divide and rule strategy.

The most important point worth mentioning is that this origin of a Munyarwanda has no scientific justification. Physical features of any people cannot be of historical reference. A discussion held with Rwandans with a progressive outlook gave a different view about the origin of a Munyarwanda. They say that Rwandans, who still adhere to the colonial and neo-colonial history of Rwanda, are apologists of colonial oppression, and that they have been disarming the people and the awareness of the source of the current state in which they find themselves.

It is suggested that only a progressive outlook can explain the causes of Rwanda's horrifying situation, which can be traced from the politico-economic causes. It is claimed that what is not known, with accuracy, since it has been obscured by authors of the history of Rwanda, is the approximate time when human occupation of the area took place. It was stated that because of anthropological findings, today we more or less have a picture of how early Banyarwanda organised themselves in production.

The same progressive thoughts assert an evolutionary concept that a Munyarwanda emerged as a production of natural properties, to start his struggle against nature, first as a single person, later in family groups and much later in larger communities. This has taught the emergency of a Munyarwanda, from the realm of natural necessity, to his free movement, from the development of brain power, to his thinking and conscious ability. His fashioning of tools gave him the ability to interact and to develop a mode of living and social organisation.

In the 1960s, Professor Walter Rodney of the University of Dar-Es-Saraam, wrote in his book, *How Europe Underdeveloped Africa*, of the nutritional climate that made Banyarwanda different.

COMMUNAL ARRANGEMENT

The early historical account of community formation in Rwanda shows a large number of groupings that characterised the communities as early as the year 25 A.D, including:

•Abashambo – Abasigi – Ababanda

•Abagesera – Abahuku – Abongera

•Abazigaba – Abahuma – Abahonda

•Abasindi – Abarega – Abasinga

•Abahinda – Abahondogo – Abacyaba

•Abenengwe – Abaha

Anthoropologists have traced the roots of human beings from 17 million years ago. They gave the following stages of man's growth and development.

SCIENTIFIC TITLE	YEARS OF AGE
Savapithecus	17 million years ago

Afaransis	5 million years ago
Africanus	3 million years ago
Homo habilis	2 million years ago
Homo sapiens	35,000 years ago.

If it is true that the origin of man was on the African continent, then it would be unjustifiable to talk about Africans originating from Asia as a red race. Scientists say that if Homo sapiens are the ancestor of man, then an estimate that Banyarwanda were grouped into large communities in the year 25 A.D, would be an accurate historical probability, given the fact that Central and Eastern Africa, where Banyarwanda inhabit, is the cradle of humanity.

Progressive historians say that the historical process is characterised by stages of development and that classes emerge on the historical scene and after outliving their role, they disappear, to be replaced by new classes relevant to the needs of that epoch. Communities refer to the primitive epoch as classes, in the sense that everything they possessed was a common property and each community worked according to its necessity.

The first Banyarwanda communities lived by hunting for food and later rudimentary cultivation. These activities were seasonal and did not guarantee food. Cattle-raising came as a better activity, but because all the communities could not raise cattle, some members of the communities had the opportunity to keep cattle. Those few Banyarwanda who kept cattle enjoyed a better means of life and were therefore looked up to by those who were still hunting and cultivating. The communities' leadership emerged as a result of cattle-raising.

Leaders of communities were elderly heads from cattle-keepers, except in communities in which cattle were not a measure of survival, like in some regions of the north of today's Rwanda.

Regions that were said to be Hutu kingdoms included:

- Nduga
- Marangara
- Bukonya
- Kingogo

- Buhanga
- Bushiru
- Kibali
- Bwishaza

- Bugamba
- Buhoma
- Rwankeli
- Budaha

The growth and development of communities amongst early Banyarwanda was not because of the number of Tutsi Hutu leaders of the time or the emergency of an exploiting class, but the phase and the struggle against the realm of necessity had been reached. The state formation was not a concentration of commercial interests. Neither cattle-raising nor cultivation was a commodity production, but more a means of survival. There were no conflicting interests between communities, because the relationship between cattle-owners and cultivators was not based on plunder.

COMMUNITY LEADERSHIP

The community leadership in the early state formations amongst Banyarwanda were made up of both Batutsi kings and Bahutu kings until the early1880s. In 1962, the Ministry of Education of the Habyarimana's regime, published lists of the kingdoms of Bahutu and those of Batutsi. The publication claims that up to 1920, during the Belgian rule, some Hutu kingdoms still existed. The aim of teaching this false history of Tutsi domination was the machination of ideological Hutu in response to the questioning of Tusti presence in the region. The author's discussion with political analysts threw some light on the question, that the Tutsi-Hutu phenomenon in the Great Lakes region was a social economic reality, before the invasion of colonial rule.

The author learnt that in Europe, slavery was a phase of development that negated communal arrangement. It grew as a result of the dissolution of the natural communal economy and it transformed small-scale production into large-scale production. It increased production and the organisation became more and more complex. The complexity of commodity production was uneconomical, and it was brushed aside by feudalism as a consequence, although it was later revived after the discovery of what was called the new world, when the African slave labour became essential for the development of America and the West Indies.

Feudalism then witnessed immense development and ushered in a dynamic economic system. Nevertheless, feudalism in Europe was characterised by imprecated extravagance. Kings and queens surrounded themselves with hangers-on and pages. Like slavery before it, it created seeds of its own distinction. Commodity production had developed aristocratic and noble classes. It was characterised by land appropriation and an international trade, by the time it was brushed aside by the new emerging system made up of industrialists, traders and craftsmen.

In Rwanda, commodity economy was non-existent and state-formation therefore had to reflect this. Territorial conquest was not aimed at increasing production, but at expanding influence. Historians have estimated that the year 650 A.D may have been the time of Gihanga's reign. What is certain however is that the phase took hundreds of years in its formative process. Apart from the Gasabo kingdom of Gihanga, a number of other principalities, such as the following, are identified:

TERRITORY	COMMUNITY
Mubali	Abasinga
Gisaka	Abagesera
Bugesera	Abahondogo
Nduga	Ababanda
Bungwe	Abenengwe
Bugara	Abacyaba
Bugoyi	Abarenge
Bwanacyambwe	Abongera
Ndorwa	Abashambo
Burwi	Abarwi

- Biyoro Bya Kabeja
- Mushongore
- Nsoro
- Mashira
- Samukende
- Nzira Ya Muramira
- Jeni Rya Rurenge
- Nkuba
- Gahaya Ka Muzora
- Nyaruzi

The intention of the list is not to organise Tutsi, Hutu or Twa community formations, but is to point out some specific instances, indicating phases of development the societies passed through. The Buhutu principals undeniably existed side by side with Batutsi monarchies, but it must be understood as a historical process, originating from the communities' means of livelihood, as nothing can come out of nothing.

It is said that the Gihanga kingdom and many others who reigned after him, remained in the Buganza province until Ruganzu I Bwimba started the crusade of conquering provinces ruled by the other leaders. Historians say that Ruganzu did not conquer territories such as Bugesera, Mubari, Gisaka and others in the north. Later, Mibambwe I Mutabazi invaded a larger territory of Nduga. However during Ndahiro II Chamatare, the state of Nduga was invaded by Abashi and they occupied it until Ruganzu II Ndahiro Ndoli ya Ndahiro, who had taken refuge in Karagwe, organised a battle against Abashi, and his victory expanded Rwanda up to Lake Kivu.

It also believed that Kigeli I Mukobanya in 1450, conquered and united Rwanda as she was found by Germany's Andrew King, who historians refer to as Cyilima Rujugira, in around 1640. He was the seventeenth king. Kigeli III Ndabarasa had a palace in the Kabungo

Ntungamo district of today's Uganda. The last king of Rwanda was Kigeli IV Rwabugiri from 1853-1895.

The writers of Rwandan history call Rwabugiri the Great Conqueror and the most active and conscious king, who fought in many parts of the region and who had extended his influence up to Lake Victoria at that time in Rwicanzige.

It said by some writers that Rwanda was a feudalism system by the time the Germans had invaded the country. But we have been of the view that the system was a mere monarchy, still at its formative stage because conditions for feudalism were not present. No accumulation of social surplus to spark off the development of feudalism had taken root. It was still a natural economy that was dependent on activities that were seasonal and quite unreliable.

An important aspect of the pre-colonial history of Rwanda is what has been termed as property relations among cattle-keepers and land holding contracts among cultivators of land. It is said that after 1870, during King Rwabugili's reign, land was divided as freehold ownerships, known as Ubukonde and Ibikingi. Some people saw that Ibikingi increased the pressure coming from the political authority on the inferior and middle social classes and that it also contributed to the strengthening of ethnic feelings, both at the top and at the bottom of society. This observation is said to be very objective as far as social classes in pre-colonial Rwanda are concerned.

The confusion on the issue of classes in pre-colonial Rwanda arises because of failure to comprehend the extremely important issue of society development. We know that our ancestors organised themselves on the basis of communal owners of land: primitive society was classless, because no exchange of goods between casts for surplus existed. The only trade between cattle-owners and cultivators was for mere survival, not for appropriation.

Communal life does not disintegrate because of state formation, but is negated by commodity production and trade. It is commodity production that created social classes in countries within Europe and North Africa. Classes were referring to those produced and those who lived off the labour of others. In Europe, prior to commodity production, captives from wars were just killed. When commodity production needed free labour to expand production beyond consumption, captives were directed to productive work. This is a testimony of the level of the Rwandan society, as found by colonialists on arrival.

A Munyarwanda had primitively struggled against nature, first singly and in families, and much later in community leadership formations. Rwanda history writers, who refer to social classes in the pre-colonial epoch, are apologists of the colonial machination and oppression that have deprived people of the knowledge of the causes of their sorry state of affair. This is not refuting the status of the monarch and the existence of chiefs responsible for various assignments. They were not an economical class, since commodity economy was non-existent by the time colonialists invaded Rwanda.

THE COLONIAL EPOCH

THE GERMAN OCCUPATION

Colonialism was economically and politically termed by the president of the U.S.S.R (known as the Great Lenin), as the highest capitalism and that politics was its highest concentration in colonies. Colonialism was said to be a direct outcome of contradictions between socialist-communists (capitalists). Colonisers justified their colonisation as the mutual advantage of both the coloniser and the colonised. It was argued that colonisation benefited the colonisers because they acquired raw materials, free labour and a market for exports to the colonised. It was also argued that colonisation was a civilising system that brought education, a modern way of life, technology and so on.

The merciless destruction of the indigenous political-economic establishments, the disruption of people's culture, the toiling of people under inhuman conditions and the pillage of the resources, meant nothing. Brutalisation of the colonised were strategies to teach colonised people submission. In the final analysis, an African was exploited but not helped and since Africans were treated as less than human, the proposition of allowing indirect rules to Africans was out of the question. Rwanda is a clear example of presumed indirect rule. It shades clarity on the mission of the Germans and later Belgians in Rwanda.

After the Berlin conference, in which Africa was shared between European countries, Rwanda became a fief of Germans from 1884 to 1919. Many Historians say that the Germans exercised a passive indirect rule and that they ignored local politics. Some went to the extent of saying that Germans were manipulated by the monarch and his high dignitaries and that his chiefs were left with more centralisation and annexation of Hutu principalities that increased Tutsi chiefs' powers. The analysis of colonisation of Rwanda by Germany is very unfortunate because the observation lacks politico-economic and even cultural views of the mission of colonialists.

A progressive political analyst once observed that when colonialism set foot on a colony's soil, it totally destroyed the power of local authority. How the Germans came to Rwanda from Tanzania and how Rwabugiri received them is not essential, and it has been narrated by many writers. The essence of history is why they came to Rwanda and to Africa in genaral.

It is also said that, at the advance of colonialism, Tutsi had a feudal system based on cattle, and they numbered only 15% of the whole population. I don't believe this – it is a number used for political reasons. A contradiction also arose when the colonial advance interrupted any natural social evolution that might have moved towards ethnic equality. We have thoroughly dismissed the erroneous assumptions that Rwanda was its mode. Our prose of human development has brought attention to the fact that our ancestors had attained cattle-ownership and cultivation just for survival. There was nothing to promote ethnic inequality since no classes had developed, because activities for livelihood were purely natural.

We have also emphasised that without commodity economy, no conditions for feudalism and classes had emerged. The monarchy and its chiefs attained from social organisation that the two major activities which had entrained Rwabugili's government, was not made up of economic class rule. Although the Tutsi (cattle-keepers) were dominant in the arrangement, Hutu (cultivators) were also in post of the administration. It is said that during Rujugira's reign, a number of Twa (the hunting group) were appointed to leadership positions. Rwabugili's leaders of the armed force were a mix of the castes. Some leaders, such as the following, have been mentioned as top senior officers in the army, of that time:

OFFICER'S NAMES OF LIVELIHOOD CASTLE

- Bisangwa Wa Rugombituri – Umuhutu
- Nyiringango – Umututsi
- Kiroha – Umutwa
- Bikotwa – Umuhutu
- Nyandera Rutuku – Umututsi
- Basebya – Umutwa
- Rukara Umuhutu
- Rwanyonga – Umututsi

This shows the social organisation of Rwanda under a kingdom that was at its formative stage, rather than a feudal system with class stratification. This book gives us the formative stages of the kingdom before colonial annexation.

The first phase that was made is of the early kings. Dates of the first Rwandan king are not well known, but according to historians the rough estimates are:

Ndahiro I:c 1350-c 1386
Ndoba :c 1386-c 1410
Samembe:c 1410-c 1434
Nsoro:c 1434-c 1458
Ruganzu I: 1458-1482
Cyirima I:1482-1506

2nd phase
Kigeli: I: 1506-1528
Mibambwe I:1528-1552
Yuhi I:1552-1576
Ndahiro II: 1576-1600

3rd phase
Ruganzu II: 1600-1624

Mutara I:1624-1648

Kigeli II:1648-1672

Mibambwe II :1672-1696

Yuhi II: 1696-1720

Karemera: 1720-1744

Cyirima Rugwe II : 1744-1768

Kigeli III: 1768-1792

Yuhi III:1792-1830

Mutara II :November 1830-1853

Kigeli IV: Rwabugili 1853-1895

Mibambwe IV: 1853-November 1896

Yuhi IV: November 1896-12,1931

Mutara III: November 12,1931-July 1959-Janury

Kigeli V: July 1959-Janury 1961.

As mentioned earlier, an overview of the political history of this type does not require a narration of how their kingships were organised, but the overview based its presentation on facts. It asserts that, before colonisation, Rwanda was struggling against a hostile environment and in its formation stage, aimed at the realisation of human potential.

It is said that there existed personal dependence, known as Ubuhake, in Rwanda before and during colonial intervention.

Some are completely ignorant of the historical motion of society and have been alarmed at the ironclad form of quasi-slavery, that enabled the Tutsi to exploit the down-trodden Hutu during the two epochs. Most of these writers, however, apart from their disastrous myopic assertion, have been victims of colonial manoeuvres, aimed at dividing the colonised people. What must be remembered is that without a Munyarwanda moving from a natural society to a commodity society, without productive labour becoming commodity and, henceforth, without a Munyarwanda selling his labour, in order to satisfy his other natural needs, there could be no exploitation of a Hutu by Tutsi. This is the situation in the politico-economic senses. This is what colonialism found on arrival: a system based on survival.

This book is unique from many other books, which were written about Rwandan history. This is because most of the other books only taught us one thing: colonial authorities worked hand-in-hand with feudal authorities. This book, however, has been based on facts: since the Germans could not be resisted, as Rwabugili's spies reported, a tactical compromise was agreed upon by Rwabugili and his top helpers. The compromise was an organisational strategy that saved the situation.

Where kings organised resistance against colonial invaders, the consequences were disastrous. When Rwabugili died in 1894, he was replaced by his son, Rutarindwa. But it is to be remembered that the Germans had already set foot on Rwanda's soil. Some Rwandan historians say that it was traitorous to accept colonialists. It is vision-lacking to say that Rwabugili had to fight colonialists and it is said that Rutarindwa opposed to the compromise. When he was made a nominal king, he thought of organising a resistance against the Germans. An agent clique was contacted to get rid of Rutarindwa and his followers. This is how the urucunchu program took place, turning the people against each other. This was a well-known strategy of colonialists: divide to rule. It is hard to accept the view that colonialists were not involved in the massacre and that it was a struggle between clans. It is not convincing to talk about political power during colonial rule. Colonialism is a politico-economy systematic, with strategies of penetration and domination, in order to exploit the colony. Rwanda was not an exception, suffice to say that the program was instigated by the Germans, to get rid of the group opposed to their colonisation and to create an agent clique to supervise their newly acquired fief.

When busy organising their colony of Rwanda-Urundi, the war between colonial powers, historians have said that the battle of Uvira between German and Belgian troops from the Congo was a determining factor which made Rwanda-Urundi jump from the German colonisation to Belgian, so-called "trustship".

A Pan-africanist writer, Professor Ngugiwa Thiongo of Kenya. said that the church was a "spiritual police of colonialism". The German church in East Africa accompanied colonisers. In 1879, the Catholic Church had set missions in Tabora Tanganyika. In 1990, Mgr Hirth of the White Fathers, established the Rwandan mission. Protestant missionaries had also established their churches in Zingi, Kilinda, Rubengera and Remera before their world war in 1914 to 1918. They left with their colonial co-workers in 1922 and were replaced by Belgian missionaries to carry on the mission. Other churches came to Rwanda later after the transfer of Rwanda from German to Belgian, from 1919. A decade of German domination was purely colonial, contrary to what many historians want us to believe concerning ethnic problems in Rwanda. They wrote how they wanted it to be known.

THE BELGIAN COLONISATION

It is said that, like the Germans, the Belgians inaugurated a colonial policy of indirect rule in their newly acquired territory of Rwanda-Urundi. The Belgians adopted a policy of "wait and see" until their trust-ship was made official by the League of Nation mandate in 1919. In Congo, the Belgian colonisation began in 1885, and Congo became a personal fief of King Leopold II. Rwanda-Urundi became a territory of the Belgian Congo in the 1920s. Frantz Fanon contributed to the deeper understanding of colonialism. He said that "domination and dependence were affected, not only through physical oppression, but through the realisations and appreciation of the manner in which the beliefs, values, attitudes, goals and aspirations of the colonial power, come to be shared by the colonised people, and this, becoming part of Africa's mental and thinking apparaties".

He continued to say that the psychological victory of the colonialist is a strategy to achieve a full political victory. Indeed, Fanon gives us a correct view of colonialism. A system, whose purpose is to dominate and alienate the colonised, in order to plunder the resources, can never be passive and indirect. By looking attentively at the socio-economic and political variable of the Belgians, we are able to demystify the view of the indirect rule of colonialists.

The first colonial governor of Rwanda was Charles Voisin. He introduced what was termed a new colonial policy: "*les reformes*". Voisin spent time soul-searching in order to decide how to behave towards the whole Tutsi complexity, instead of the system of indirect rule bequeathed by the Germans. It is said that Mgr. Classe of the Catholic Church, acted as political consultant to the Belgian administration to take Batutsi as an element of progress, saying that: "The greatest mistake the government could make would be to suppress the Mututsi. We will have no better, more active and more intelligent chiefs than the Batutsi. They are the best ones suited to understand progress and the ones the population likes the most. Therefore, the government must work mainly with them."

It is said that the advice prompted the colonial administration to fire Hutu chiefs and to replace them with Tutsi ones. It is a process of socio-economic and political journey of any society, still at its primary phases, that a leading measure of survival becomes a basis for leadership in social organisation. In Rwanda, colonialists found that cattle-keeping could guarantee the survival better than the remaining of activities, which were seasonal and could not be reliable. It was upon that economic set-up that the Rwanda kingdom was based.

The Rwandan feudal system had not acquired the capacity to shift from a nature level to a commodity society. There was no capacity to produce a social surplus up to the time the country was invaded by colonialism. Historians have been praising the Rwandan kingdom for rejecting slavery practice. It does not mean that Rwanda's pre-colonial leaders were a special type of people, it simply means that the level of economic growth and development had not attained the production capacity to generate surplus and to employ or sell labour. Analysts have also been talking about corvee labour, known as *uburetwa*; about selfdom in the form of *ubuhake* slavery; about land ownership in the form of *ibikingi* and other forms of exploitation. It said that Belgians encouraged and multiplied these institutions. These observations by authors and historians leave a lot to be desired. They are expressions of sentiment, lacking in both content and form. This book, on the contrary, is based on facts. Such facts can serve to put clarity on the real and genuine trend of politics and economics of Rwanda found in the country by colonialists.

In most parts of Africa, including Rwanda, the conditions for feudal development were not present when colonisers invaded these parts, since the accumulation of social surplus was not large enough to spark off such development. By the time Africa came into contact with Europe in the seventeenth century, before formal colonisation, feudalism was already relegated to the museum of history and it was impossible for it to strike new roots. The Tutsi, Hutu and Twa casts found in Rwanda and in the Great Lakes of the continent were economic groupings of cattle-keepers, cultivators and hunting stratum, indicating an economy of simple reproduction, basically rural and quite natural, without having acquired the capacity to produce a social surplus. While colonial administrators and their propagandists viewed Rwanda as a land of unequal distribution of resources, we see Rwanda from an emerging communal, social organisation, to a political society, but still based on natural economy. Division of labour into productive and non-productive strata was not based on large-scale production and investment, but rather on a non-productive group of owners of cattle and land, whose business was simply warfare and public affairs, and on the activities of grazing cattle and cultivating land, simply for consumption. The points served as an eye-opener to the question of exploitation of Bahutu by their Batutsi lords. The *ubuhake* was termed an unequal client-ship contract. Some analysts see the patron-client relations as more visionary than those talking about Tutsi cohesion of oppression.

One of the divided and rule strategies of the Belgians was to institutionalise the traditional social cohesion of Tutsi-Hutu relations into a feudal French type of 1789. It was presented as an evil form of exploitation contracts. The chief was instructed to develop the client-ship and land tenure contracts. Rwanda, however, rejected or resented the contracts because they realised that it was imposing a foreign way of life. In what was termed the fundamental re-organisation of Rwanda, the Belgians entrusted the Catholic Church with almost all functions, including recommending the appointment of chiefs. It was termed reorganisation because King Musinga and his chiefs had uncompromisingly objected to Belgian administration and to the evangelisation of the Germans, and some of his men had fought for the Germans. Musinga had also rejected the Christianisation of the country, even during the German occupation. Missionaries reported to the new Belgian administration that he had totally refused to be converted to Christianity, and that he hated the Belgians. In reality, he did not hate Belgium but he did not want to be colonised by foreigners. (Prunier: 1995,30.)Frantz Fanon has taught us that in order to score a political victory, the colonialist had to first achieve a psychological victory. This teaching explains why Musinga had to pay a heavy price for his rejection of Christianity. He was accused by missionaries of having rejected the civilising mission, and for this reason was openly hated by the church.

On the advice and recommendation of the Catholic Church, the Belgian authorities banished him into exile, in Congo. The church was overjoyed at Musinga's banishment, and had already made plans for his replacement. This forced exile of King Musinga was a political indicator that two systems cannot co-operate. It then reminds us of an ideological analysis that once colonialism sets foot on a colony's soil, it destroys the power of the local rulers.

The Belgians together with the Catholic Church had already consulted some anti-Musinga chiefs who recommended Rudahigwa, Musinga's son, for the responsibility of supervision. In 1934, Rudahigwa was given a nominal throne with a title of Mutara III. His enthronement was not even accompanied by traditional rituals. To Rwanda, Mutara Rudahigwa was a king of the whites (Umwami Wa Bazungu), however, for the church and the administration, he was a bridge to converting and transforming the Rwandan society. Up to 1920, Christianity had not spread, owing to the resistance to conversion by Musinga and his associates. The few converts were those Rwandans who thought that they would benefit from it, and other Rwandans considered them as traitors. After Rudahigwa's appointment – not enthronement – a mass of conventions were a great delight to the church, since they were only contented with the social outcasts, who used to be their only clientele, immediately after the appointment of Mutara. Father Soubielle declared the enthronement of what he called, "a massive Catholic army". Another missionary wrote that the natives of Tutsi's conversion were questionable, but with the help of God, they would become good Christians.

On the administration aspect, both central and local authorities were strictly Belgian: the governor general was based in Leopoldville. He was responsible for both Belgian Congo and Rwanda-Urundi. The so-called trusteeship of Rwanda-Urundi was delegated to the vice governor in charge. During the German rule, Rwanda had its own governor residing in Kigali. As Belgian colonies or trustee territories as they were called, their chief administrators were known as residents in Usumbura.

In Rwanda today, provinces, formerly prefecture, were known as territories. The country was administratively partitioned into:

- Astrida or Butare
- Kigali
- Nyanza
- Byumba
- Kisenyi
- Ruhengeri
- Kibungo
- Cyangugu

It can be noted that each territory was strictly ruled by an administrator and his assistant, and the two positions were held by Belgians only. Each territory had sub-territories known as territorial agencies. An agent of the territory acted as an overseer, under the assistant administrator. All agricultural, veterinary, medical and educational personnel were Belgians.

The reason for listing these colonial administrators is to expel misconceptions that Belgian colonial agents ruled Rwanda indirectly, leaving all the powers to the *umwami* (king) and his Tutsi chiefs. The king or *umwami* had no authority. He was nominally supposed to have authority over chefferies and sous-chefferies. The chiefs and subs were appointed by the administrator and parish priests to head of mission in the area, and the only role played by the king was to approve the choices.

The church, as a french historian remarked, became all things to all men. In 1945, Mgr. Classe was said to be a national monument with monopoly in education and the medical service. It is said that since Batutsi were natural born chiefs, they monopolised education. Rene Lemarchand wrote in his book, *Rwanda and Burundi*, that Hutus had to go to theological post-secondary institutions, such as seminaries, because they could not be enrolled in administration colleges, such as in the Astrida (now Butare) group of seminaries and they could hardly find employment.

To explain what many analysts term the marginalisation of the Hutu by the Tutsi, is absolutely indispensable to acquire the concept that colonialism was exported to colonies. It is important to study influences of colonisation as a strategy for domination. Simple education was a superstructure of the system. I have dismissed propositions that Tutsis were direct rulers of Rwanda, because colonialists were indirect and passive rulers. Education was geared towards the accomplishment of the mission. It would therefore be redundant to talk about Hutu marginalisation, instead of talking about the strategy of divide and rule that was applied to Rwanda-Urundi.

Many writers have correctly referred to the Catholic Church as the main social institution in the Rwandan society from 1932. It is even said that by the 1940s King Mutara III Rudahigwa had become a pearl of great price and that he even consecrated the country to Christ the King in 1946. He did this in recognition to the transformation that had taken place in the country. This book, however, has learnt that, on the contrary, Mutara Rudahigwa developed an antagonistic relation with quite a number of very powerful priests, and Rudahigwa made the offer to their bishops. The offer was reported to the Vatican and a medal of appreciation was sent to him, through the bishop. Later, Rudahigwa applied for the transfer of those priests and they were immediately recalled. This strategy was a victory to Rudahigwa. Some people think that offering the country to the Catholic Church was tantamount to auctioning it. Others see the move as patriotic and a sign of political maturity. But due to political opinions there was no way Rudahigwa could be a darling of the church and their colonial co-operators, because he had no say and authority. His father was banished to Belgian Congo and the church had become all things for all men, as the saying goes.

From 1920, Belgians introduced what they termed reforms, to create what they were calling modern Rwanda. Taxation, forced labour and other colonial activities, created anti-Belgian feelings among the people. Brutal beatings brought created an exodus towards Uganda, where there was plenty of unforced work. Gerald Prunier, a French historian, wrote that "the Tutsi, superior race may have shown all power at the centre, but made up for this by monopolising local administration and contractual means of economic control".

This view is lacking a politico-economic analysis. It failed to grasp the meaning of power at the centre. Political analysts refer to state power as a state made by a committee with an ultimate authority and forced to run the affairs of a ruling class. A ruling class is a social stratum of production and in command of superstructures of society. It is the ruling class that holds the power of the *umwami*. There was no central and local authority in Rwanda. The ruling class was in Belgium. The local authority was the government class from the government down to the territorial agents. The *umwami* and the colonial chiefs were mere serfs, supervising other serfs. They were neither the ruling class nor the administrating class. Contractual economy (*ubuhake*) is dispelled by the type of economy found by colonisers in Rwanda.

The *ubuhake* arrangement was simply for survival based on caste crossing from cultivation to cattle-keeping. Of course, the mission of colonialists had to be put into practice by dividing the colonised people in order to accomplish its objective. Rwanda had no race, no tribes, no ethnic differences, and the Catholic Church had an evangelisation monopoly. Apart from the castes of survival, nothing else could be a base for dividing Rwanda. Contradictory statements show that the question of client-ship had been negated by money. Gerard Prunier said that cash economy introduced, in Rwanda, had made the old client-ship system absolute. It is very true that monetisation integrated all the activities into colonial economy.

This fact has been overlooked by writers of the history of Rwanda. Instead, they have been talking about a superior race, a high caste, the Tutsi elites and other terms, aimed at inciting the Hutu caste that they were oppressed and exploited. This book has commented on colonial education to create what they were calling elites. The majority of Batutsi students were found in Astrida's group of colleges, and most Bahutu students were in seminaries. This so-called education was aimed more at ideological than career training.

Mgr. Classe died in 1945 but left a legacy of keeping Bahutu out of what he called the "structures of the country". He said: "some missionaries would like to see Bahutu reigning one day, especially Christian Bahutu there would be a revolution."

After his death, the church became very busy; creating what was called a Hutu counter-elite strategy, where church leaders decided on the policy after seeing that Batutsi priests were influential even in the church itself. European church leaders, in agreement with the colonial administration, started to create Hutu elites as early as 1947, after the Second World War. At the same time, Rudahigwa and his associates started attacking the Belgian administration for failing to provide basic needs to Rwanda and, instead, being pre-occupied with fermenting divisions among Rwandans. It is said that several memorandums were secretly dispatched by Rudahigwa's close associates to the trusteeship council. The confrontation sharpened the contradiction between colonial authorities and the people's representatives.

In the early 1950s, Rudahigwa made a tour of Europe and took that opportunity to expose the machination of the Belgian administrators in Rwanda. The move was seen as a colonial challenge by the king and his followers, and since the gap had been dug, the colonial authority had to resort to the division.

THE NATIONAL QUESTION

In colonies a national question was essentially the principal and central contradiction, which refers to the principal enemy in a given colony. In Rwanda, the monarchy had died when colonialism interrupted its formative process, because its material foundation had been completely destroyed. The existing relations had been eliminated, as well as the power of the king, turning the kingship into an instrument to advance the colonial mission. The primary contradiction became sharper, when the kingship and his aids started consultations with other African leaders.

In the early 1950s, Rudahigwa made a stop-over in Cairo, Egypt, to seek advice from President Abdul Nasser of Egypt, on his way to Belgium. It is said that he made several visits to Uganda to consult the *kabaka* (king) of Uganda, and some Ugandan Banyarwandas, as the famous nationalists John Karekezi and Frank Karimuzo among others. He also had political discussions with Julius Nyerere, who was then a university lecturer at Makere University in Uganda.

Realising that the client-ship, or *ubuhake,* was to be made a basis for dividing the population, Rudahigwa requested for the abolition of the *ubuhake* relationships. The Belgian authorities allowed him the abolition of the relations. It is important to remind the reader that the client-ship contract was not based on commodity economy, but was a contract for more survival. It said that Rudahigwa wanted an electoral system and the creation of a local council of representatives. He wanted popular elections of the country chiefs and their sub-chiefs. The proposal to create a representatives council was granted by the colonial authorities, but elections of representatives were rejected.

On another political front, Mgr. Perraud, the most powerful agent of the colonial administration, was busy organising what was known as a council of old seminarians. The council was strictly a Hutu organisation. The decree, which allowed the creation of councils by the *umwami* (king), was later amended by the colonial authorities, and authorised the *umwami* to nominate a representative, which included Hutu representatives. Europeans in the church opposed the inclusion of Hutu councils. They thought that the inclusion of Hutu elite groups, in the council, was an additional challenge to the control of the country, since the first challenge was that of appointing a Tutsi bishop and Tutsi priests as leaders of a number of parishes.

The church had earlier created an organisation of propaganda. One of the instruments was a newspaper known as *Kinyamateka*. It became the most read paper in Rwanda, under the management of Gregoire Kayibanda who later became the president of the country. He was also the owner of *L'ami* (*the friend*) from 1952-1956. When the agricultural cooperative Trafipro (Travail Fidelite Progres) was created in 1956, Kayibanda, its chairman, still acted as chief editor of *Kinyamateka*. In various parts of the country, Bahutu Evolues were instructed, by both the church and the colonial administration, to start organising their Hutu people, creating cultural associations, based on mutual assistance between members of clans such as: Abasinga, Abagesera, Abashambo and other clan groupings, but the plan was immediately repudiated by the colonial authorities.

In March 1957, a group of the so-called Hutu Evolues, published a tract note on the social aspect of the race in Rwanda. The tract, better known as Bahutu Manifesto, voiced the humiliation and socio-economic inferiority of the Hutu. Earlier a group of colonial administrators called liberal Batutsi, headed by Bwanakweli Prosper, had been formed. The two main groups were set up to serve as anti-nationalism tools. It is believed that the manifesto was planned and engineered by Mgr Perraude's office. In part, the manifesto talked about the Tutsi rule. The problem was basically that of the political monopoly of one race, the Batutsi. The political monopoly had been turned into a socio-economic monopoly and given the facto selection in schools, a cultural monopoly had been added, which condemned Abahutu to be forever slaves of Batutsi. In order to monitor the race monopoly, Hutu were opposed to remove the ethnic origin of people (Tutsi, Hutu and Twa) from identity papers.

The other problem, according to the Hutu Manifesto, was the monopoly of power by the Tutsi. The declaration was made by Hutu elites on the instigation and order of the colonial authority, through the Catholic Church. This analysis was called devilish and deviant. The economy was purely colonial and a political power, while in colonial Rwanda, it was the concentration of capitalism. I have dismissed the race propaganda in Rwanda as a demagogic delusion. The Hutu manifesto provoked reactions from the group that was pro-Umwami. The group condemned the Hutu group and the Bwanakweli group, calling them tools of colonial manipulations. A number of Tutsi notables, claiming to be the Umwami subjects, also reacted to the manifesto saying that: "as things stood, then, there could be no fraternity between Hutu and Tutsi". This is because of sharp contradictions both primary and secondary, which became a turning point in the struggle for independence, and the alarming crisis in the country. I think it is irrelevant to go into detail of the exchange of words from the two sides. The national question, therefore, although not applicable in the African conditions, was everywhere: the conflict between colonisers and the local leaders.

THE INDEPENDENCE MOMENTUM

The demand for independence in most Afrian countries, including Rwanda, gained momentum in 1957, as soon as Ghana attained its independence. By this time, many liberation movements were very active. Rwandan leaders, with Rudahigwa as head, thought that it was the right moment to wage their struggle for self-determination. They decided to take the opportunity to create a unity because of liberation struggles. Other colonies had exposed the incapacity of colonisers to keep their colonies by force. Rudahigwa intensified his consultation with nationalist leaders in Uganda, and held several discussions with Julius Nyerere of Tanganyika, and other Ugandan leaders such as Kabaka, Patrice Lumumba of Congo. He also made an agreement with Prince Rwagasore of Burundi and had a discussion with nationalists from Ghana, Guinea and Egypt.

It must be recalled that from 1950 up to 1954, Japan and the USA lost the battle and war against North Korea, helped by the people of the Republic of China. The victory of communism thus created an engulfing crisis throughout the capitalist world, including colonies. Visionary analysts have said that, when colonialism was faced with an engulfing crisis, it crushed whatever appeared to be a barrier to its domination and continuation. The struggle for independence, therefore, was an engulfing crisis to the Belgian classical colonialism in Rwanda. As a counter-reaction, the Hutu Manifesto was followed by the formation of a proper political party, in May 1957. Its leaders wrote a letter to the vice-governor about what they termed the Hutu-Tutsi problem.

The Hutu leaders who signed the letter included:

- Maximilien Niyonzima
- Gergoire Kayibanda
- Claver Ndahayo
- Isidore Nzeyimana
- Carl lope Mulindahabi
- Godefroid Sentama
- Silvestre Munyambonera
- Joseph Sibomana
- Joseph Habyarimana Gitera

The association of the promotion of the masses was the brain-child of Mgr. Perraudin, the Bishop of Kabwayi and the adviser to the Belgian colonialists in Rwanda. To the Belgians, the promotion of the Hutu caste was a counter-revolution, since the down-trodden Hutu oppressed and exploited by the Tutsi as a colonial machination, aimed at turning the people against the other. The mass, according to political analysts, refers to economic classes. Questions one can ask here are: were there classes in pre-colonial and colonial Rwanda? Was there antagonistic contradiction in colonial Rwanda? Who was the real enemy of the people of Rwanda during the colonial epoch? The answer to the pre-colonial situation is a simple no – classes exist in commodity. The society, in capitalism, is divided among the haves and the have-nots. The masses are the toiling have-nots, selling their labour in order to the haves and to earn a living.

Since colonialism set foot on the colony's soil, it completely destroyed the ruling powers. In Rwanda, conditions for the development of feudalism were non-existent when colonialists invaded the country. There was no vision in talking about promoting the mass, when the society was still living on the mercy of nature. Another issue is about antagonistic contradictions in colonial Rwanda. In any colony, the primary and principal contradiction is colonialism. The secondary and non-antagonistic contradiction is the castle factor of Hutu-Tutsi. The *umwami* and his chiefs, as previously explained, were mare serfs, supervising other serfs, the enemy of the coloniser, no more no less. Talking about black colonisation is myopic and vision-lacking.

Many writings and a number of letters, re-written by Fidel Nkundabagenzi in his book *The Politic in Rwanda*, are a testimony of the colonial mission in Rwanda – the letters including Maus' letter to the vice-governor. Maus was a member of the colonial council. The letter of 25th April 1956 talked of Bahutu becoming conscious of their inferiority on the social aspect. The governor's reply on 27th April commended Maus' analysis saying that it was quite incontestable. On May 7th 1956, Munyangaju Aloise wrote to Maus, praising him for his support to the Hutu cause. Similar letters exist to date, clearly sharing the political crisis that had engulfed the country.

On the political front, on the side of the nationalist, it was in the same year, 1956, that Rudahigwa was frequently visiting Kampala, in Uganda, for political advice from the *kabaka* of Uganda and Ugandan nationalists such as John Karekezi. Aprosoma's action programme was published in 1958. Munyagaju outlined the position on what came to be known as the Hutu movement.

ON ETHENIC GROUPS

The programme talked about complementarities between Batutsi, Bahutu and Batwa. It was said that if the Belgians did struggle with the monopoly of one race (Batutsi) over other races (Bahutu and Batwa) it would be a key to finding the solution of the Tutsi-Hutu problem.

ON THE RWANDA – URUNDI STATUS

Aprosoma proposed a federation between the two countries. Kirundi and Kinyarwanda were said to be already one language and the French language was proposed as a complimentary language, after independence.

FEDERATION OF CONGO, RWANDA AND BURUNDI

Aprosoma's declaration said that the Tutsi regime had subjected the country to an ideology of racial superiority. That bias has to be rectified and Aprosoma proposed a federation between the three countries, as opposed to the wishes of Bututsi, who wanted the federation with Uganda because they had dreams of establishing a hamitic empire. For instance, they had kin in Ankole, Toro, Bunyoro, and Buganda.

THE WHITE / BLACK RELATIONSHIPS

The declaration condemned what it termed the Batutsi's bution to the country's civilisation. Batutsi wanted Britian or Germany to replace the Belgians, the statement said.

INDEPENDENCE

Aprosoma's statement said that Batutsi were "running up and down, seeking support for independence from UNO members". Some Bahutu elites have conditioned that independence needs the establishment of solid democratic institutions first. Aprosoma demanded equal opportunities for all. Aprosoma's declaration also contained its strategies for economy, land reform, education elections, the formation of government and of the legislative council, and other political issues.

The struggle for independence in many countries was a historical process arising out of a desire for a people's self-determination. The struggle for juridical independence was waged by all, in an attempt to solve a national question. A national question is a historical phase, concerned with the right of people for self-determination. During the struggle, efforts were made by the colonialists to channel the strugglers to their use. Failure to secure their objective, colonialists looked for alternatives. That was the case in Rwanda. Aprosoma was an alternative to Rudahigwa's group.

THE DEATH OF RUDAHIGWA

It is a well-known strategy of colonialists that once they control a colony, they do not relinquish it, until it is smashed by independent forces, or to crush those agitating for self-determination. That was exactly what took place in Rwanda. On 25th July 1959, Rudahigwa was murdered by Belgian authorities. According to Mr Runuya Selevilien, who accompanied him to a meeting of African nationalists in Burundi, Rudahigwa was called by his so-called "personal physician" from Pagidas Hotel where he was waiting for a delegation from Ghana, Mali, and Guinea. On arrival at the doctor's clinic, he found there were eleven Belgian Comandos waiting for him. The commandos drugged him with a poisonous chemical and he died on the spot. The same white man who had called him from the hotel, went back to call his delegates. Mr Runuya went with him to the clinic, only to find Rudahigwa's dead body on the floor. Surrounded by the eleven commandos, Mr Runuya went back to report to the delegation the death of Rudahigwa, still in the company of the same white men. The delegation from Rwanda left for home immediately to organise the burial and to inform the public. The Belgian plan to pre-empty the arrangement for independence, by the Belgian authority, was tried when the vice-governor general of Rwanda-Urundi brought Mr Makuza Anastase to Rudahigwa's burial to introduce him to the care taker, until a new Mwami was nominated and approved by the Belgian authority. All Rwandans present at the burial widely protested. The governor had to give up the decision, and allowed Rwandans to declare their new king. Michel Kayihura, who was very close to Rudahigwa, announced that Mr Jean Ndahindurwa had to be the new *umwami* of Rwanda. Ndahindurwa was given the title of Kigeli V and he was Rudahigwa's brother.

Makuza Anastase was one of the best cadre of Belgians. In June 1957, Makuza and Kayibanda were assigned the responsibility of forming a movement known as MSM (Movement Social Hutu). The movement had a mission of mobilising and inculcating sectarian Hutu, ideological in the minds of the Hutu caste. But because the principal economy was already known, the ideology failed. A political analyst once said that people were ignorant of what was going on, but they were not fools. Apart from the few tools of colonialism, such as Makuza, Kayibanda, Bwanakweri, Gitera and company, the whole population at the time, were behind whoever claimed to be anti-colonialism.

After King Rudahigwa's burial, the Rwandan crisis became more and more engulfing. As a result, UNAR was declared on the 3rd of September 1959. The party was formed by Rudahigwa, before his assassination in May 1959.

UNAR (RWANDAN NATIONAL UNION)

According to a number of writers, UNAR was a monarchist movement, anti-Belgian and a Tutsi conservative party. However, Rwandans who have keenly followed Rwanda's political developments, have dismissed this view saying that UNAR had a nationalist character and its manifesto proved that. The manifesto contains its stand on independence and its rejection in being used as a tool of neo-colonialism, later, after independence. The composition of UNAR's leadership proved that it was not a Tutsi movement, as it was composed of all ethnic backgrounds. Its president was Mr Rukeba Francis and its secretary general was Mr Rwagasana Michel, who was Kayibanda's cousin. At its inception, UNAR's leadership was made up of the following:

- Francis Rukeba
- Michael Kayihura
- Michael Rwagasana
- Cosmas Rebero
- John Rwangobwa
- Peter Mungarurire
- Clever Bagiiashya
- Jovitas Nzamwita
- Austin Mutabaruka
- Silver Bulingufi
- Vedast Ntarugera
- B. Nyanzunga Anzunga

Some of the fundamental principles of UNAR included:

THE DOCTRINE
In principle, UNAR's charter stated: UNAR rejected any collaboration with the colonial authority. It condemned the colonial manoeuvre of dividing the people into non-existent races of Tutsi-Hutu and Twa. On collaboration, UNAR compared Tutsi-Hutu colonial manipulation in

Rwanda with the South African racial policy, and with the condition of Black Americans, in the USA. UNAR disassociated itself with any Rwandan advocating for, or suggesting a flexible stand in dealing with the colonial authority. It vowed to oppose any traitorous compromise with the enemy. UNAR pledged moral support against Kaburu (colonialist) in South Africa, for the Mau Mau of Kenya, called saboteurs by colonialists, condemned the confrontation between Bakongo and Kasai, and that of Lulua and Baluba in the Congo.

POWER STRUGGLE

UNAR planned to establish democracy based on parliamentary representation. It wanted a constitutional king and an executive premier, as the head of government. The declaration separated powers into executive, judiciary and legislative.

LEGISLATIVE POWER

In its manifesto, UNAR proposed:
- Direct free elections
- Determination of the nationality status
- Establishment of local councils

JUDICIAL POWERS
- Establishment of a judicial commission
- Establishment of the structure of the courts
- Codification of national customs and merging them with good laws
- Formation of judicial cadres to assist professional legal staff

EXECUTIVE POWERS
- A constitutional king as a head of state to be endorse
- An executive prime minister chosen by Parliament to be elected
- Appointment of cabinet ministers and their assistants by the premier
- Appointment of chiefs and sub-chiefs to work councils

ECONOMIC POLICY

UNAR believed that political emancipation had to be accompanied by socio-economic and even cultural emancipation. UNAR felt that economic planning was a means of avoiding wastage.

Its planning contained the following, among many other provisions:

- Rationalisation of trade and commerce.
- Exploitation of natural commerce.
- Industrial establishment, development.
- Establishment of rural cooperatives.
- Creation of large farms and small scale enterprises.
- Investment attraction and tax policy formulation.

FORMAL EDUCATION

UNAR's plan for national education focused on:
- State orientation and participation in education of a national university in Astrida with all the faculties.
- Civil education to all pupils and students in all the schools.
- Formal education of cadres with the aim of creating manpower.
- Development of a new national culture in all aspects of life.
- Articulation of rights and civil liberty of every one.
- Establishment of centres for the eradication of illiteracy and as information media.
- Setting up youth centres and National Service Institutions, as capacity-building schemes.
- Setting up professional and technical colleges to supplement education.

RELATIONS IN THE COUNTRY

UNAR was gravely concerned with contradictions created by colonialism in the country, between Batutsi and Bahutu. For UNAR, independence was not aimed at kicking out Belgians and other Europeans. It was merely aimed at self-determination. UNAR wanted justice and mutual understanding and respect.

RELATIONS WITH OTHER COUNTRIES

UNAR considered the union between Rwanda and Burundi to be of vital benefits to the two countries. It was proposing a future confederation between the two, depending on mutual agreements. UNAR had proposed economic cooperation between Rwanda and Anglophone countries of Uganda and Tanganyika. Its international cooperation envisaged the respect for Rwanda sovereignty, legitimate right and mutual advantage, with all countries they choose to.

CONCLUSION

UNAR concluded its declaration as follows:

- That UNAR was not a mere political organisation, but a movement with a strong national vision to achieve total emancipation and liberation.

- That UNAR appeal, to the colonial authority for its demands, to be taken into account.

- UNAR condemned the malignant colonial divide and rule policy of racial problems in Rwanda. The conclusion made an appeal to the people to join UNAR, as a union, in its struggle, to liberate and construct a peaceful Rwanda, characterised by a national harmony.

The above were some of the important declarations of UNAR. It was claimed by both the Belgian authority and the Catholic Church leaders, that UNAR was getting finances and diplomatic backing from Communist countries and that much support deepened antagonism between UNAR and the colonial administration.

According to UNAR founder-members, political analysts and many Rwandans, it was about political movement. During the colonial era, a number of knowledgeable Banyarwanda's were convinced that UNAR was a nationalist movement as the time dictated. They are saying that today, nationalism has attained an ideological proportion, quite different from the view of the independent pioneers. They are crediting UNAR for its organisational structure of a national, not sectarian, character. They are equating it to other nationalist parties in Africa like Nyerere's Tanu, Rwagasore's Uprona, Obote's UPC, Lumumba's MNC, Kenyata's Kanu and many similar African parties, with a nationalistic form. The 1950s and 1960s were years or decades of antagonistic confrontation between communism and capitalism. Communist countries found it an ideological obligation to support liberation, independence movements and parties, not only in Africa but all over the colonial and Non-colonial world.

What is known, as we shall see later, about relation or support UNAR scored from communist countries, is that it got their support in the 1960s when it was presenting its dependence claim to the UNO, and after its independence was hijacked by Belgium and handed over to her "stooges": USSR, the people's Republic of China, Albania, Cuba and Bulgaria.

An argument about the UNAR's feudal character has it that there could be no feudalism during the colonial era and that the monarchy, which existed in pre-colonial Rwanda, had been crushed by colonialism because its material foundation had been destroyed. That, after all, by the time colonialism invaded Rwanda, as mentioned earlier, conditions for feudalism had not developed.

Another picture given to UNAR was that it was a party of Batutsi with a racial bias. The leadership and *raison-d'etre* of UNAR, however, have proved the contrary. It was the only union with a national perspective and programme.

UNAR's hostile attitude towards the Belgians, claimed by many writers on Rwanda, was justifiable since it was a nationalist party, with its main objective of winning unconditional independence. For Belgium, independence meant a loss of colony and influence, which was intolerable. The vice-governor general wrote in his book: "the agreement which the admistration had made in the 1920, with the

Tutsi ruling caste, in order to further economic development, was allowed to collapse. The Tutsi wanted independence and they were trying to get it as quickly as possible by sabotaging Belgian actions, whether technical or political. The Belgian administration was forced to tonguing its attitude towards that hostility and obstruction coming from chiefs and sub-chiefs. Harroy with his authority was forced with a crisis. Toughening his attitude meant crushing the uncompromising UNAR. To counter UNAR's independent wind, Chief Bwanakweri was told to form a political part."

LE RESSEMBLEMENT DEMOCRATIQUE RWANDAIS OR RWANDA'S DEMOCRATIC UNION

This party was formed in September 1959. Because of its colonial administration support, the party became unpopular among the Rwandan population. It was the colonial strategy to create a Tutsi movement, in order to weaken UNAR's popularity. Bwanakweri's lack of popular appeal to the people caused his down-fall, and like Gitera of the Aprosoma, he was left out in the cold. Later, he joined UNAR in exile and decided to return to Rwanda. Together with UNAR members who had not fled the country, they formed an opposition. In 1954, Bwanakweri was killed with others, accused of treason.

THE BIRTH OF PARMEHUTU

It is important to emphasise on the primary and principal contraction in any colony, because in Rwanda, the secondary and non-antagonistic contradiction between the people themselves was shielded by the colonial authority, to cover their strategy to retain the colony at whatever cost. The secondary contradiction was the Tutsi vs. the Hutu colonial creation. The capitalist law of accumulation provides that a colony must be reformed to become a neo-colony, should independence claim gather momentum. In the 1950s, the war in Korea: USA and Japan against USSR and China, in which USA and Japan were humiliated and lost the war, created a terrible crisis to colonialism. That is why Belgium was determined to stop any group that intended on inflicting a humiliating defeat to its direct and indirect perpetual occupation.

UNAR's uncompromising resolve and lack of support were a basis for advancing what they had earlier termed the Hutu cause. To toughen its attitude against the hostility and obstruction of the Tutsi, as disclosed by Jean Paul Harroy, the vice-governor general for Rwanda-Urundi, a secondary contradiction already created, had to be shielded. This contraction came in the form of a Hutu movement. It must be remembered that the movement had been waiting in the wing of the Catholic Church for an opportune moment.

In May 1959, the Hutu movement, a creation of Mrg. Perraudin of Kabyayi, had written to Harroy, and the governor guaranteed them support. Under the instigation of the church, the Hutu group released its action programme on 9th October 1959. The programme summary includes:

- Parmehutu's general policy
- Its foreign policy
- Its education programme
- Wearth distribution

GENERAL POLICY

In the manifesto, Parmehutu asserted that it would create a genuine unity of Rwanda, by abolishing what it termed subjugation of one race by another (Hutu by Tutsi). It said that it was aiming at instituting a real democracy in its future government and in the economic sector, which had been all monopolised by the Batutsi.

Parmehutu vowed to fight what it termed colonisation of the

Buhutu by the Batutsi, through servitude and forced labour. It totally rejected independence without abolishing colonisation of the Hutu by the Tutsi.

It saluted the effort of Belgium to civilise and develop the country that was being changed by Bututsi's. It wanted the democracy first, followed by a national referendum, to ask the people whether they wanted independence or not, because the Belgian authority had joint strategy with the Tutsi to colonise the Hutu!

ORGANASATION AND ADMINISTRATION.

Parmehutu proposed a new structure of administering the country, for the duration of at least seven years, before holding a discussion about the country's independence. His proposals included the creation of prefects in the head of prefectures under Belgian administrators, who would replace the white administrators later. Instead of having territories, there would be the abolition of providences and establishment of communes to replace locations. A constitutional king adhering to the democratic aspiration of Parmehutu. A resident elected by a national council and acting as an assistant to the white resident. Election of the prefects by the councils also to act as assistant to the white administrators. Bourgmestres as head of communes elected for a three year term and responsible to the white administrators. National legislative assembly and prefectural and communal houses.

FOREIGN POLICY

Parmehutu had plans to enter into a commercial and financial agreement with Congo (DRC) and Tanganyika (Tanzania). It had a plan to set up a Rwanda – Urundi council, and the Belgian governor was to remain the overall authority until the two countries became independent. On the proposal for federation, Parmehutu was to fight for freedom first, before considering the integration with countries of the Central African Region.

EDUCATION PROGRAM

Parmehutu had a plan to educate all non-advantaged children of Rwanda (Hutu) by introducing technical education for children who would not qualify for secondary education. It would allow private schools to operate freely. Since Hutu children could not afford to pay for boarding, Parmehutu would abolish all boarding schools. Identity cards indicating the cast group would be introduced to know Tutsi and Hutu children.

INDEPENDENCE

Parmehutu rejected independence that would favour the Tutsi. Chains of servitude and forced labour imposed on the Hutu by the Tutsi, should be broken first. It suggested an arrangement to culminate the subjugation of the Hutu by the Tutsi, and proposed:

- A reasonable period of political, judicial and educational democracy
- Distribution of land and wealth equitable between Tutsi and Hutu.
- Election of the king and doing away with his nomination by the abiru.

Some of the resolutions above, extracted from Parmehutu's manifesto, are very educative. They tell us that what happened in the 1994 genocide was pre-arranged by the colonial authority, using its compradorial agents so that its continuity was guaranteed. The declaration talked about subjugation of one race by another.

The pre-colonial epoch was a primitive era in which people were struggling for more survival. Rwanda was made up of cattle-keepers and cultivators. Since the economic life was natural, there was no need to talk about relations of production. Exploitation took place in a class-stratified society, with the haves exploiting and oppressing the have-nots. Before colonialism in Rwanda, the natural economy had not even developed conditions for feudalism. Rwanda's kingdom was merely paternalistic.

When colonialism set foot on Rwandan soil, the administrative structure that was emerging was negated by capitalism and it was colonialism that introduced forced labour and servitude. As a colonial tool, Parmehutu had to blame the victim because it was a strategy of the colonisers to turn the colonised against each other. Otherwise, no explanation can be given to the subjugation of a serf supervising another serf! A few Bututsi colonial chiefs were merely supervisors – they were not rulers at all. Musinga was handcuffed and taken to the Belgian Congo as a prisoner. Rudahigwa's cold-blooded murder by the colonialists, earned him a title of a nation hero.

Permehutu insisted on a genuine democracy first before demanding independence in a colony. Democracy for whom and by whom? That is why I refer to various systems of democratic governance later. Parmehutu blamed the Belgian authority for jointly colonising Bahutu and Batutsi. Colonialists did not come to Africa to look for friends, they came to plunder resources and to turn the continent into a fief for capitalisation of their capital. Administrators came to colonise; religious people came to educate; and explorers came to discover new lands and opportunities.

The book already has brought to the attention of the reader the cause and effects of colonialism. In other countries, homage is paid to heroes who fought for independence. However, of course, Parmehutu was a *parti du movement et de l'emancipation*. It is to be remembered that, as far back as 1912, Mgr Classe, the then head of the Catholic Church, had made plans for what he called a social revolution. It was then time to effect the plan.

On 1st November 1959, a member of Parmehutu's executive

committee, Mr Dominic Mbonyumutwa, organised the massacre of all Tutsis in his Ndiza area; he was a sub-chief in the province. Some observers I have contacted gave me reasons why the Tutsis had to be exterminated. A more convincing reason was that the colonial authority had tried to recruit elites to be their agents after independence, but failed. They recruited chief Bwanakweri, but found that he was not popular like UNAR leaders. It was said, the de facto leader of Chief Kayihura Michel was on several occasions, approached by the resident of Rwanda and the vice-governor of Rwanda-Urundi himself, but Kayihura refused to be used.

It is a well-known strategy of colonialists everywhere, to try to channel nationalists to constructive use and failure to turn them into instruments to advance their own interests. After the Ndiza and Rubengera massacre of UNAR supporters, using Parmehutu, Belgium decided to replace the resident with a soldier.

On 4th November 1959, Colonel Guy Logiest was detached by General Janssens from the Belgian base in the, then, Belgian Congo. In his book *Mission Au Rwanda*, Logiest shows how he came to play the role in Rwanda. He says: "Some among my assistants thought that I was wrong in being so partial against the Tutsi and that I was leading Rwanda on a road towards democratisation and was distant and uncertain! No, the time was crucial for Rwanda. Its people needed support and protection. My role was essential and it was important that I could play it till the final verdict would come from the communal elections. Today, twenty-five years later, I ask myself what was it that made me act with such resolution! It was, without doubt, the will to give people back their dignities and it was probably just as much the desire to put down the morgue and expose the duplicity of a basically oppressive and unjust aristocracy."

Logiest's statement dispels any hesitation and denial of the colonial manipulation. The 1921 social revolution planned by Bishop Classe had reached its climax. His partiality meant that Belgium was determined to retain the country at any cost. Colonialists cannot lose their fief, unless smashed by liberation forces. He said that the people of Rwanda needed support and protection. By the people, the colonel meant the Hutu caste. They were made to believe that they were the majority. In a colonial setting, there existed the relations between the coloniser and the colonised. The relationship is that of domination, dependence and exploitation.

This book has repeatedly referred to the pre-colonial economy as purely natural and primitive. It was the industrial revolution of 1780 in Europe that developed production and accumulation. The struggle was not a Tutsi vs. Hutu struggle, it was a national self-determination of an engulfing, cruciform colonial authority. It was the year of independence for Belgian Congo. Patrice Lumumba invited the exiled King of Rwanda and members of UNAR to the independence celebrations. Belgians could not stomach this alliance. The authorities organised another massacre throughout the country. Many refugees went to Uganda, Tanzania, Burundi and to the Congo.

Radio Vatican called the killings the "most terrible human massacre, similar to that of Jews by Hitler." Even Bertrand Russell commented on the killings, calling them the "most systematic human extermination we have had to witness since that of Jews by the Germans".

In December 1960, UN resolution numbers 1579 and 1580, condemned Belgium's policy in Rwanda. The UNO authorised Belgium to organise what it called a "national reconciliation". Logiest called the request useless, and instead, he called Kayibanda and other Parmehutu leaders, including 3125 Bourgmestre to an urgent meeting, on 28th January 1961.

Logiest declared that Rwanda had become a republic. This meeting came to be known as the Gitarama Coup in 1961. He ordered the remaining Batutsi's in Rwanda to be in the Bugesera area. Systematic killings were once more carried out and more people took refuge. Logiest immediately organised what he called "democratic election". Few supporters of UNAR remaining in the country were persuaded to participate in the election. Parmehutu was declared the winner with 78% and UNAR was given 17%. After the officialisation of Parmehutu, UN made a comment on the election of Rwanda that:

"an oppressive system had been replaced by another one," and that it was "quite possible that some day, violent reactions would be witnessed on the part of the Tutsi". The UN comments implied that the Hutu oppressive system would replace a Tutsi oppressive system, and that another violent reaction against the Hutu system on the part of Tutsi would take place.

According to my political analysis, it is the politico-economic within that people refer to as the Tutsi feudal system within a colonial system. (Colonialism was termed the highest stage of capitalism by Lenin of the USSR.) Even backward economies were integrated to capitalism not to talk about natural economies, like Rwanda's communal economy. Domination and dependence were strategies to achieve the objectives of colonialism. Monetisation of African economy, trade and investment made colonies totally integrated and dependent. Talking about the oppressive system replacing another similar system, therefore, has no politico-economic content and even form. Colonialism, instead was characterised:

- By toiling under in human conditions
- By pillage of resources
- By barbarism and brutality
- By depriving the colonised image of self and pride
- By reducing the colonised people to utter wretchedness
- By disrupting the culture of the colonised people and giving them a colonial one.

The UN predicted a reaction on the party of the Tutsi. The leaders of UNAR had shown that it was not a party of Tutsi, but a union of national character, representing a principal resistance aimed at self-determination.

The Hutu falsity was advanced to shield colonial manipulations. There was nothing like the Hutu action and Tutsi reaction, but there was a national union of Rwandans to struggle for independence. It was true that the Belgians' massacre had to be resisted, but the resistance was aimed at Belgian authorities. It was not a resistance against the Hutu as some writers assumed.

THE INYENZI AND ITS RESISTANCE

An attempt by UNAR leaders to get independence was a terrible blow to the status quo of Belgium. The leaders had foreseen the danger of playing into the hands of a merciless colonialism. Some had organised the youth, in exile, to struggle for independence from the early 1960s. The resolution could not get unanimously granted independence to Rwanda in 1962, as per UNAR's application. To the Belgians, what was important was not granting independence to Rwanda, but who would be the leaders of an independent Rwanda. Parmehutu had already been propelled to the compradorial leadership; a factor that could not be swallowed by UNAR leaders. They organised an armed resistance and made contact for training the youth.

It was not easy to get concrete information about the Inyenzi. The name, which means cockroaches, was an abusive language used by Parmehutu, as an instrument of propaganda, against the freedom fighters. The propaganda was that Inyenzi were a mere nuisance, homeless and useless like cockroaches. Colonial authorities in Rwanda and their Parmehutu, claimed that Inyenzi were bands of terrorists aimed at sabotaging the gains of the 1959 social revolution. Many Rwandans, even today, thought that Inyenzi were groups created by leaders who had no political orientation. Supporters of the monarchy thought that Inyenzi were fighting to restore Rwanda's monarch, dethroned by the colonialists. UNAR leaders claimed that Inyenzi were their youth movements, resisting colonial manipulations. Some Inyenzi leaders who are still alive, are still asserting that some of the groups were liberation movements guided by progressive principles. Other sources think that Inyenzi lacked a subjective initiative and were unable to continue the struggle. A Ugandan minister of defence Mr Mbabazi, wrote in the *New Vision* Ugandan newspaper, that Inyenzi in 1960s, lost the bottle because they had no external support, unlike the Inkotanyi (RPF) of 1990. Rwandan nationalists saluted Inyenzi and their leaders for organising resistance movements, against one of the most horrible colonial systems, witnessed in the 1950s–1960s in Rwanda, irrespective of Inyenzi's ideological limitations and external conditions for their successful resistance or liberation.

WHO WERE THESE INYENZI FIGHTERS?

As mentioned earlier, it was not possible to know the structures of the various groups exactly. The first Inyenzi group, under the leadership of Kayitare Rubeka, son of Francis Rubeka and Numa Mpambara, started in the 1960s, and many of its leaders were killed by the Belgian authorities and, later, by the Kayibanda regime. The group led by Nyabujangwe and Kayitare, attacked Gabiro in Umutara, Musha, Kigali rural, and Kanzenze in Bugesera.

The Inyenzi killed many Belgian agents, destroyed Belgian installations and disarmed a military unit in Bugesera. They passed through Burundi and Tanzania, and they went to Uganda. Another organised group was the first Ingangurarugo, led by Nzamwita Jovite, and named after the famous Ingangurarugo division of King Kigeli IV Rwabugiri, before the colonial invasion of Rwanda. This group was based in the Congo and were operating in the Ruhengeri and Gisenyi provinces, later, the group was reorganised under a new leadership of John Rwangombwa, Ngurumbe Aloys and Kayitare Masudi. Ngurumbe had been trained in China. The group even participated in the Congo, helping Jean Piere Mulele.

In Uganda, the Inyenzi were reorganised by a certain SaibaA, who had also been in China's leadership and was later taken over by Wereabe Canisius, who had been in China for military training. Their leadership was later taken over by Canisius Wereabe, who had been trained in China as well. Werabe and his men attacked the Umutara in 1964 and were defeated by a combined force of Belgians and Rwandan troops. Webare was killed together with his commandos, such as Rutagengwa, Nyanzinge and others. In Burundi, a National Liberation Front was formed, under the leadership of Gabriel Sebyeza, a former Bwishaza chief and UNAR representative to Tanzania and China. The F.L.R formed an alliance with the old Ingangurarugo, after Mulele signed an agreement with Mobutu but, on arrival to Kinshasa he was killed. The F.L.R (Front de Liberation du Rwanda) was the most organised front. It was said that the front had a leftist inclination. Apart from Sebyeza, other leaders of the alliance included John Rwangombwa, Ngurumbe who was the leader of the front's military wing, together with Masudi Kayitare and Gakwaya, who was its chief coordinator and had been to Cuba several times for military assistance and ideological consultation. Young intellectuals like Munana and Bucyensenge also belonged to the front's leadership. The front's struggle ceased in 1967, when the Burundi government became hostile and arrested its leaders. Kayitare Masudi was killed by an army officer of the Burundi armed forces, while Sebyeza and Rwangombwa were expelled, and went to Uganda. The second famous group was M.P.R(Mouvement Populaire Rwandais). The movement was led by Joseph Mudandi, a Chinese trained fighter, who had also participated in the Congo liberation struggle. The movement acquired arms from the Congo and crossed to Bugesera through Burundi, and destroyed a military camp at Nkanda. The movement ceased to fight in 1967, also as a result of Burundi's hostility to Rwanda's liberation movements. The colonial situation always offered a historical opportunity of organising a struggle against colonialism. Because of their subjective position during the colonial time, UNAR leaders were able to organise resistance movements, but because external conditions were not able to sustain, they concluded the struggle. UNAR leaders were divided probably because of discouragement and the lack of financial support. Some were based inside Rwanda, thinking that they could constitute a powerful opposition. They even participated in the so-called elections of 1962 and Michael Rwagasana and Prosper Bwanakweli decided to join the break-away group in Rwanda.

RWANDA'S INDEPENDENCE OR DEPENDENCE ?

In Africa, the end of direct and classical colonisation, in most countries, was realised in the 1960s when colonies became sovereign entities, in the political sense. Politico-economic analysts said that colonialism changed its form because the struggle waged by African independence leaders was a liberation movement, resulting in the weakening of colonial domination. The decline of imperialism was caused by the challenge mounted by socialism, and the forces of equality and justice in imperialist countries themselves. Some socialist countries have given their support to Africans, in their struggle for self-determination. Therefore, self-determination was the preliminary victory scored by the leaders and independence was recognition of the democratic right of African nations. Indeed, the question of self-determination was partially solved because it was scored at least on the formal political level, even if the fundamental economic rights were not granted. As a result, the political independence became a short-lived euphoria. It was soon noticed that classical colonialism was replaced by neo-colonialism. Financial dependence or finance capital had to continue, mediated by an agent class. Some were looking for a model to follow, but not all models were right for Africa. For example, the independence a la Latin America developed a number of problems. For instance:

- The problems of development strategies to be followed

- The problem of political direction and institutions after independence

- The problem to have a state structure for the country to replace the colonial state

A country is not independent when its relations with or to colonial economy remains subjugated to that economy, even after political independence, monetary dependence, trade dependence and lack of development of man's physical, intellectual and psychological assets. The concept of dependence, thus, lies on the forces of dependence, domination and neo-colonialism. This is the continuation of the colonial system. One of the well-known nationalists in Kenya, Mr Oginga Odinga, wrote a book and called it *Not Yet Uhuru!* He was referring to Kenya's total dependence under Jomo Kenyat's presidency.

The transfer of colonial rule to an agent class, in the neo-colony therefore, was a plan by any colonial power, in order to keep the country in direct check. This was exactly the case in Rwanda. As said earlier, what was of essence to Belgium was to leave the country to an agent class. Colonel Logiest said: "Rwanda's nominal independence was celebrated on 1st July 1962. This is the time when alarmed all African leaders were talking about moving to the left. Some countries like Algeria, Guinea, Madagascar, Tanzania, Ghana, Benin, Congo and many others, went as far as calling themselves socialist states. Even criminal fascists, like Mobutu of Zaire, had resorted to revolutionary slogans." (Logiest:1963.)

For Rwanda, nationalism was out of the question. Kayibanda and company were praising Belgium and singing what was termed a social-democratic revolution by Colonel B.M. Logiest. Kayibanda was a creature of the Catholic Church. As expected Kayibanda's slogans were that democracy had taken root in Rwanda. It is often said that Kayibanda applied the same system of leadership to that of the king. In this book I have repeatedly dismissed this misconception and said that after the invasion of Rwanda by the Germans, during the reigning of King Rwabugiri, the monarchy was destroyed by colonialism and other kings, who had replaced him. The question of becoming a king of the Hutu did not arise. It is a known strategy of colonialists that they continued ruling through an intermediary class, linked economically as the former coloniser, and had the second highest share in Rwanda, almost equated to that of Belgium!

Many historians, who have been analysing the trend of events in Rwanda, have been expressing their surprise at Kayiabanda's silence, when most of the African leaders were talking about moving to the left. For intermediary agents of Belgium, in Kigali, anti-colonialism was out of question. Nothing is surprising about the silence of agents in Rwanda. In the book, *Rwanda: du Feodalisme a la Democratie*, Jean-Paul Harroy, the then vice-governor general of Rwanda-Urundi, dispels the surprise, describing his visit to Kigali for the tenth anniversary of independence. He saluted the heroes' welcome he and Colonel Logiest received.

What authors refer to as the Rwandan ideology after independence, are democracy and republicanism. All songs on the national radio were praising democracy and democracy meant that Rwanda was ruled by the Hutu majority after crushing feudalism in the 1959 revolution. Republicanism meant that Rwanda had merged from feudalism to a republic. It was indicated that the only form of struggle possible in the 1960s was that of independence. This book has also indicated how and why efforts were made to make nationalists intermediaries and that failure to tame them, created what Rwanda experienced in both 1959 and 1994. For Kayibanda, the only values to be emphasised on were the intrinsic worth of being Hutu.

Dependence and under development were not a problem. It was said that what was important was the dignity of a Hutu, in an atmosphere of freedom from the bondage of a Tutsi. In her book, *La Sociologie Des Pasion*, Claudine Vidal wrote that: "After independence, Rwanda slowly turned into an island: the government feared its whole environment: it was horrified by the Congolese rebellions, reserved towards Tanzania, hostile to the Tutsi regime in Burundi and dependant on Uganda's roads for its imports. The inhabitants were inward-looking and bore the country's slow shrinkage in silence. There were several forms of censorship: from a triumphant Catholic church and from the government which was afraid both of possible communist-inspired movement and of the traditional manifestations, which could be a reminder of the Tutsi imprint, which it considered something like phobia. To the government, lack of trust, rumour, secrecy, lack of breathing space on top of material deprivation. The country was one of the poorest in the world and lacked almost everything." (Vidal:1965.) Obviously Vidal's observations are a manifestation of Rwanda, as a fief of Belgian and other partners, after independence. Claudine's analysis was not able to look at the causes of the regime's horrific situation. They say that Kayibanda and company were employed to act as a barrier to any structural change and to preserve domination. Rwanda became an island, as mentioned in the quotation, which was a direct result of the pressure mounted by liberation movements, which had been formed in exile since 1960, when Rwanda was still under the direct control of Belgium. My comments on the Inyenzi operations have clarified why the regime had to be socialist, and were jointly struggling against both the Kinshasa and Kigali regime. This is the reason why Claudine said that the regime was horrified by the Congolese rebellions. They were not in fact rebellions, but rather a liberation movement. They did not succeed because of many conditions, including subjectiveness, which were not in their favour. The idea that the regime was reserved towards Tanzania was very true. Tanzania declared its move to the left in the early 1960s, followed by Uganda. The Arusha declaration and the Nakivubo pronouncement were all anti-imperialism. There is no way, therefore, that Tanzania and Uganda could cooperate with a country lead by people like Kayibanda.

As for Habyarimana's Rwanda, it had been geared towards serving and preserving dependence. It was a good observation to say that the people in Rwanda were inward-looking. It is a general historical condition of any society to be inward looking. Sooner or later they discover the difference. That is why they required a subjective initiative to get them out of their miserable state. Such initiative, as we shall see later, is very hard to come by. We cannot blame the victims as they had to bear the shrinkage in silence.

The "Tutsi phobia" as Vidal said, was a part of the Rwandan ideology. The Tutsi phobia, as seen earlier, is as old as the colonisation of Rwanda itself and this was the result of misconception of people living in Rwanda. Tutsi were neither a class nor a tribe. They were a caste of survival whose means of livelihood were better than those of the Hutu stratum. Because of that, they became community leaders, from which kingships emerged. Kings resisted colonialism and as a result, plans were made to either use them as agents or to exterminate them. The latter was resorted to both before and after independence. In 1961, even Radio Vatican called the extermination, "the most horrible human massacre, similar to that of Jews by the Germans."

Between December 1963 and January 1964, more than 50,000 Tutsi's, together with a few Hutu supporters of UNAR, were slaughtered on the pretext that they were supporters of external liberation movements (Inyenzi). Many prominent leaders, such as Prosper Bwanakweli, leader of Rader, Michael Rwagasana, the secretary general of UNAR and others, were killed. Because of Belgium's instigation, no foreign reactions to the horrible killings were voiced. It was simply termed "Inyenzi terrorism" by the puppet regime, and this situation has never been revised to-date. Writing about the Rwandan ideology, Jean-Pierre Chretien said that: "since independence, Rwanda had steadily followed the policy of ethnic quotas."(Chretien: 1970.) He stated that there were officially 9% of Tutsi's in Rwanda, and so there could be no more than 9% in school, or in any given sector of employment. Parmehutu claimed that the Belgian colonial authorities had exercised partiality in education and employment by favouring the Tutsi. Jean-Pierre Chretien wrote many books about political developments in Rwanda. His analysis of Rwanda's political developments, however, have been totally rejected by Rwandans who have been following political events of Rwanda.

The policy of quotas, of the Tutsi-Hutu setting, was a colonial framework that divided the country when colonial Belgium set foot on Rwandan soil, and it continued to be a guiding directive, since independence up to 1994, when the most horrible genocide became its logical conclusion.

Partiality in education and employment was another view. There was no colonial favouritism. There was a divide and rule policy and it was applied everywhere. It was no surprise, therefore, that the policy was applied successfully in Rwanda, through Hutu vs. Tutsi castes; not classes or tribes. All schools in Rwanda were strictly controlled by the Catholic Church. Was the Catholic Church impartial? Did the Catholic Church favour Batutsi? Were they in favour for Batutsi? The real problems of Rwanda, this book has repeatedly put clarity on, resulted on contradiction between colonial rulers and the monarch, especially Musinga who has been an example by rejecting the Catholic Church.

After succeeding in installing a puppet clique in Rwanda, Prince Louis Rwagasore, prime minister of Burundi, was assassinated. The Hutu of Burundi were instigated to make a coup, but it was pre-empted and Hutu leaders were killed, including the prime minister, Mr Ngendandumwe. From then, the Hutu vs. Tutsi formula has been tested. To accomplish his mission, Kayibanda and company continued advancing the Hutu ideology of having liberated the country from Black colonialism of Batutsi. In exile, the total number of political refugees from 1959 to 1973, has never been accurately written. It has to be remembered that even in the pre-colonial time, Banyarwanda were citizens of the whole Great Lakes region. From 1920 to 1950, other Banywarwanda's migrated to Uganda and Congo, because of the colonial oppression.

The two political and social factors made it impossible to get statistical data of Rwandan refugees in the region. Some writers have estimated that, when R.P.F launched a liberation struggle, refugees were around 2.3 million. Others have estimated the total number to be 115,000. Writers have wrongly claimed that Rwandan migrants were economical rather than a political stratum of Banyarwanda. My view is that colonial migrants and even pre-colonial Banyarwandans were living outside Rwandan borders mainly because of political reasons, even though some exception can be found. After all, politics cannot be divorced from its economics origin.

The intermediary role of Kayibanda, therefore, was instrumental to the Hutu ideology in the region. During his years, Kayibanda extended the ideology to Burundi. Prominent Hutu politicians in Burundi like Ngendandumwe, Cimpaye and others together with Kayibanda, organised several coup attempts in May and June of 1963 and Hutu leaders in Burundi conspired with Rwanda's regime to kill Tutsi's in Burundi. The plan was discovered by Burundian government before it was put into action. The Burundian government worked on the plan. It is said that more than 10,000 Tutsi's, as an act of retaliation, on the pretext that were supporters of the Inyenzi movements, were killed. Many students, who took refuge to Rwanda from Burundi, were given free education, and the Hutu ideology was the dogman taught in school of Burundian refugees. (suggest rephrasing). People like Ndadaye, Ntaryamira and Ntibantunganya were the front-line cadres of the ideology. Apart from the anti-Batutsi slogans, the Kayibanda regime had other, but minor, contradictions of a sectarian dimension. The Gitarama group was used by Kayibanda to check on, what was termed, the Ruhengeri and Gisenyi mafia. The southerners were Kayibanda's worry as well, because they had been supporters of Aprosma of Gitera from Butare. From 1961 to 1967, the regime was littered with armed liberation movements, that it was unable to defeat, until the time when the movements withdrew to Uganda and Burundi, due to lack of external support.

THE REFUGEE FACTOR IN UGANDA

The Banyarwanda are undoubtedly the largest group in the Great Lakes region. Historically, the group is of the three castes. Cattle-keepers are known as Batutsi, land cultivators are known as Bahutu, and small caste of hunters are known as Batwa. These were castes found in the region by colonialists on their arrival. In Rwanda and Burundi, the castes were turned into races of different origins by the colonialists. The colonial policy of divide and rule was based on this social reality. In the 1950s, the independent struggle in Rwanda was turned into a Hutu revolution against the Tutsi colonisation. When Habyarimana took over the power, the estimation of Rwandan refugees was around 2.1 and 2.7 million in exile. From 1961 to 1979, several Rwandan political activities, in countries neighbouring Rwanda, were going on. Liberation movements and political parties were organised, especially in Uganda and Burundi. In Burundi, the most organised movements were Front de Liberation du Rwanda or the F.L.R (Front for the Liberation of Rwanda of Sebyeza Gabrier and the Movement populair de Liberation or M.P.L (Popular Liberation Movement of Mudandi Joseph). In Uganda, apart from UNAR's activities, Sebyeza headed P.S.R or Partie Socialist Rwandais (Rwandese Socialist Party). Later, in 1972, Mr Katarebe Joram founded the Abatangana movement to be known as Imburamajoyo, according to the monarchists.

Investigations made revealed that when Idi Amin made a coup in Uganda, in 1971, supporters of King Kigeli of Rwanda, in exile in Kenya, where he had been since 1964, organised his return to Uganda. Kigeli was given forty-eight hours to leave Uganda in 1964, by the Obote government because of his association with the Kabaka of Buganda. Many Banyarwanda in Uganda say that Kigeli became a close confidant of Idi Amin Dada. Others unjustifiably claim that Kigeli had attained the rank of an advisor. I learnt that Banyarwanda leaders had negotiated with Amin's government through Mr Wanube Kibedi, who was Amin's minister for international relations, and that a compromise was reached, to invade Rwanda. It is said that because the deal was negotiated by the anti-Kigeli group, the Kigeli group used the Baganda monarchist to hijack the arrangement. Amin was made to believe that Kigeli was the only leader who could unite Banyarwanda.

But why was Idi Amini an enemy of Kayibanda of Rwanda? When Idi Amin over threw Obote's government in 1971, he became a close associate of Somalia, and Somalia was an associate of Burundi under Michel Michombero. Rwanda was training Hutu leaders and their army to invade Burundi. In addition, Kayibanda was moving towards Tanzania because of her confrontation with Burundi.

Tanzania was also supporting Hutu movements to invade Burundi. This is because there was no Burundian refugee at this time. It was therefore an opportunity for leaders of the Rwandan community in Uganda to take advantage of the political situation in the region. The leaders discussed the invasion plan with Mr Wanume Kibedi and Idi Amin himself. Idi Amin's army was said to be the most trained and equipped in the region, stronger even than the Tanzanian forces. An intelligence report revealed that the Rwandan armed forces were between 20,000 and 25,000, while Idi Amin's was six times bigger. After drawing the invasion plan, a certain Ssarongo, who was Amin's director of national security, told Idi Amin that Banyarwanda had a de facto leader, King Kigeli, and that Kigeli was the sole symbol of unity, accepted by all Rwandans, both in and outside of Rwanda. Banyarwanda leaders who had negotiated the political compromise with Amin's government, on their part, argued that Kigeli had been a national liability, rather than being a uniting factor. In fact, Sebyeza Gabriel had disassociated himself with Kigeli, as far back as June 1964, when he wrote an article, which appeared in a Luganda newspaper, known as *Muno*, calling Kigeli a national liability and that he was nothing but an empty fat pig. The same statement is found in a book written by professor Rene Lemarchand called *Rwanda-Burundi*.

Obote's government was overthrown by Idi Amin by order of the British government, when Obote was attending a meeting for the heads of states of the Commonwealth of Nations in Singapore. The coup was welcomed by Britain, Israel, Ethiopia and South Africa. British and Israeli officers had been training Obote's army. It is said that the coup was a result of Obote's move to the left. In fact, the alliance between Obote and Nyerere was a big threat to British interests in the region. After Obote was over thrown, Amini allowed Baganda to campaign openly for the restoration of their Kabakaship. Banyarwanda monarchists in Uganda took advantage of Amini's commitment to restore Buganda's Kabakaship, after the lavish reburial of Kabaka Mutesa, in April 1971, in order to make an alliance with Baganda monarchists. They jointly arranged for Kigeli's return. However, the removal of Mr Kibed from the Foreign Ministry was another blow to the Rwandan leaders, who had apposed the invitation of Kigeli to Uganda, and his support by Baganda monarchists. However, all effort was in vain. The political situation was favouring the monarchists. Kigeli and his entourage received a warm welcome from officials of the Ministry of Foreign Affairs headed by the then minister Paul Etyang. Kigeli and his men were given accommodation in the Nile Hotel by the Amin government.

Addressing delegations from refugee settlements and from towns, in Uganda, Kigeli vowed to crush his enemies within a very short time. He later made a tour of all the refugee camps and got a jubilant welcome from huge crowds. On his return from the refugee settlements, Katarebe, Muyenzi and Sebyeza were arrested by Amin's state research men; an intelligence group that was entrusted with the elimanation of people opposed to the Amin regime. They were accused of being leaders of the Imburamajyo group; an opposition movement that had negotiated the invasion of Rwanda, by striking an agreement with the government before Kigeli's coming to Uganda. Muyenzi and Katarebe were hammered to death in the Naguru torture chamber in Kigeli's presence, eyewitnesses have revealed. Their supporters were killed in Masaka, Nshungezi refugee camp and in many other places, as it was alleged. Sebyeza and Rwangombwa and other members of their group narrowly escaped to Kenya. It is said that Kigeli ganged up with Amini's close confidants to culminate his opposition, accusing his opposition of working with Tanzania and Amin's enemies, in Tanzania to invade his regime. The point I am making is that refugees from Rwanda, especially those exiled in Uganda, never failed to reorganise their attempt to go back to Rwanda despite all the problems they faced.

THE CHANGE OF GUARD IN RWANDA

The post-colonial history of Rwanda has been a very sad spectacle, when successive regimes or the government in Kigali have been oppressive. Indeed, the 1960's genocide and its 1994 conclusion proved this. Kayibanda's regime was not over thrown by military officers because of Kayibanda's tyranny, but because he was faced with an engulfing crisis, and his mentors feared that invasion from outside could cut their links with Rwanda. Some of the reasons from the various strata of Banyarwanda were:

• That the Hutu ideology of the regime in Rwanda, extended to Burundi, could develop into a terrible and dangerous repercussion.

• That the regime had been completely isolated from regional affairs.

• That the regime was faced with an external invasion, which Kayibanda was unable to stop and that it was feared that Kayibanda could be forced to resort to Ujamaa of Mwalimu Nyerere of Tanzania.

Therefore, Habyarimana, Kayibanda's minister for defence and army commando, together with Alex Kanyarengwe and Lizinde Theonest, also high ranking positions in the Belgian-French trained army, took power in July 1973. There was nothing exciting about the change of guards in Rwanda. For the refugees, in the Diaspora, and people with conscious views of the state of affairs in Rwanda, it was rather a jump from the frying pan to the fire. In his book, the *Rwanda Crisis*, Gerard Prunier rightly wrote in 1995: "given the horror in which it concluded, there is now a tendency to project back upon the whole of Habyarimana's regime, knowledge of its ultimate evil." The horror that concluded the Hutu revolution was nothing but a mere outcome of their ideology of the 1959 revolution. The intensification of the slogans of Rubanda Nyamwinshi or the Hutu majority or Igihugu Cyacu, meant that Tutsi's were black colonisers and were given preference during the second regime.

Throughout Habyarimana's years, there was almost no single Tutsi prefect or Bourgmestre, and no Tutsi officer in his whole army. The quota system of people set up by Kayibanda was retained by Habyarimana. It was criminal for an army person to marry a Tutsi woman, at least, prohibited by laws of the army forces, and in accordance with the Hutu commandments.

It has to be remembered that Habyarimana overthrew Kayibanda when his regime was threatened by an invasion from Burundi and Uganda. Idi Amin had become a friend of Mobutu of Zaire. Mobutu took an initiative of reconciling Idi Amin with Habyarimana. Later, Habyarimana was invited to Uganda to meet King Kigeli. When Kigeli organised a party to meet some Banyarwanda in Kampala, at his Buganda road residence, I learnt that Kigeli disclosed that he had entered into a bond friendship with Habyarimana. A source close to Kigeli told me that Kigeli was rewarded two luxurious cars and an allowance of an undisclosed amount for renouncing the right to return to Rwanda. When Kigeli struck a bargain with Habyarimana, with Idi Amin mediating a settlement, many Ugandans speaking Kinyarwanda were mercilessly slaughtered. The living example is Imburamajyo people, who were killed and accused of being supporters of Museveni's Fronasa or Front for National Salvation, that had just launched an unsuccessful attack from Tanzania in 1972.

When Idi Amin outed Obote in 1971, the Banyarwanda community were the fourth largest community in Buganda. Today, Banyarwanda are said to occupy a large number among 21 million Ugandans. In the 1950s, the Banyarwanda leaders were among the front line strugglers for Uganda's independence. A large community of Banyarwanda in the name of Abadahemuka; after Mutara II Rudahigwa's army, existed in the early 1950s.

The killing of Muyenzi and Katarebe did not mark the end of the struggle. But to refugees in East Africa, it was a big blow because another subjective initiative took time to come back. For refugees in Congo and Burundi, lack of ideological consciousness and political exposure became an impediment. In Uganda, the external condition favoured an initiative, but Kigeli and his aides became a barrier to the organisation and of the movement.

THE HABYARIMANA YEARS

It is said that Kayibanda was starved to death rather than being executed because Habyarimana's superstitions feared that his blood oath of fidelity to him would cause harm. I do not agree with the superstitution. I think that Kayibanda's removal was purely ideological as earlier observed. Starving him to death was a result of contradictions among the compradorial camp. One year after taking over from Kayibanda, Habyarimana used a party known as the Movement Revolutionnaire National de development – National Movement for the Development or M.R.N.D.

The movement consolidated what many foreign authors called the Rwandan ideology. Tutsi were still black colonisers who came from afar and could not be considered as citizens. Belgium remained the main mentor of the regime. Habyarimana also became the stooge of France and Germany, and Rwanda acted as a magnet of Canada, the USA and Switzerland. In the country, however, the contradiction intensified. Kayibanda died in prison in 1976. It is said that between 1974 and 1977, Habyarimana's security chief, Colonel Lizinde, had killed fifty-six people, mostly high-ranking officials of the Kayibanda government. A minister of international cooperation, Augustin Munyaneza was said to have been buried alive. Kayibanda's removal from power was not brought about by the struggle for power between him and his high military officers. It was a plan by his Belgian mentors because of the reason earlier referred to: Idi Amin had made plans to invade Rwanda, Kayibanda was training Hutus to invade Burundi, and had supported an unsuccessful coup against Michel Michombero of Burundi. This was a Hutu coup that had been organised by Belgian security personnel and O.U.A (Organisation de l'Unite Africaine) agents, because it was alleged that Michombero's friendship with Siad Barre of Somalia, had moved him from Belgian camp to the side of the U.S.S.R.

In 1972, the coup turned into retaliation against Hutu organisers of the coup. Tanzania, on the other hand, had never recognised the

Permehutu administration because of Kayibanda's compradorial role in the region. Habyarimana, therefore, was brought to power as a change of guards to overshadow Kayibanda's actions and with an overmastering desire to make Rwanda the Catholicised nation in Africa. In fact, the Archbishop of Rwanda, Mgr Vincent Nsengiyumva, was an active member of the M.R.N.D central committee. However, the Catholicisation of the country and its direct supervision, by both France and Belgium, did not stop exiled fighting for power. It only reduced the confrontation between regime and its external neighbouring countries.

Several coup attempts and power struggles were a big threat to Habyarimana. In April 1980, Habyarimana's security chief, Colonel Lizinde, made a coup attempt, together with colonel Alex Kanyarengwe and Murego Donat, both from the Ruhengeri prefecture, now province. The coup aborted and Colonel Lizinde was put in the Ruhengeri maximum security prison together with other military officers, while Colonel Kanyarengwe escaped to Tanzania. In April 1988, Colonel Stanislas Mayuya, said to have been the choice of Habyarimana for succession, was murdered. It was rumoured that Mayuya was killed by Habyarimana's brothers-in-law, who was the state clique of his regime. It is said that Mayuya's death was organised by Colonel Serubuga, a member of the most powerful group of Mrs Habyarimana's clan. Habyarimana's close associates, such as Colonel Nsekalije, was dismissed from state organs by Kanziga's brother and cousins. Habyarimana himself originated from Kigezi in Uganda, reliable sources said.

It is often wrongly said that the political tradition of Rwanda, from the kingship to Kayibanda, and later to Habyarimana, was that of an unquestionable loyalty. This view is not acceptable. The kingship in pre-colonial Rwanda has been repeated and was a political organisation based on natural economy. When colonialists set foot on Rwandan soil, it destroyed everything, in terms of politics and economic formation. Kayibanda and Habyarimana were good boys of both Belgium and France. I cannot therefore compare an independent system, in the formative process, with a dependent system, remotely ruled by its metropolitan masters. In fact, during the fifteen years of Habyarimana's supervision, not rule, France replaced Belgium as the regime's mentor, because it offered a guarantee in everything, namely military, political, financial, etc.

In 1975, a military guarantee was made, and troops were sent to protect the regime. This was proof that Rwanda was a direct appendage of imperialism. In addition, the epoch of feudal development was over, when the bourgeoisie replaced feudalism, and ushered in capitalist relations in Europe. It is, therefore, vision-lacking to talk about traditional loyalty as a feudal legacy, when feudalism was non-existent in Rwanda and when Rwanda had became a fief of France and Belgium at the time. The struggle for power within Habyarimana's clique was a normal conflict, to take over the leadership.

Political analysts say that internal causes are linked to external conditions, and the two affect the politics within a given country. Rwanda has had its experience of this. In the1960s, the liberation movement did not succeed in removing Belgium's political watchmen, not because of their incapacity to fight them, but because of lacking external support.

In the 1970s when Kayibanda was faced with an invasion crisis, he was harried by removal by his masters. The internal conflicts within the camps of Habyarimana did not matter very much, as long as he was able to deal with threats of civil war from Uganda. His friendship with Kigeli had wrongly given him an assumption that the crisis was under control. When Kigeli took refugee to Kenya once more, after Idi Amin's regime was overthrown by the Uganda National Liberation Front (UNLF), with the help of Tanzania, he continued to receive assistance from Habyarimana, in cash and in kind, according to some Rwandan refugees who lived in Kenya at the time. Apart from a compromise with Kigeli and his group, Habyarimana and his government, on the advance of their masters, organised a resettlement scheme for young refugees in exile. Many refugees were resettled to Canada, Australia and to the Scandinavian countries. Only Tanzania rejected the plan and suggested a nationalisation solution instead of selling Africans as cheap labour.

In Uganda, the condition was different. The removal of the tyrannical regime of Amin, came with a hope for Rwandan refugees. Among Uganda's National Liberation Army (UNLA), made up of Yoweri Museveni's Front for National Salvation (FRONASA) and other smaller groups, were a number of Banyarwanda commanders. They included Fred Gisa Rwigema, a member of FRONASA's high command, who were trained in Mozambique. It is said that Rwigema was recruited by Kahinda Otafire who became colonel and minister in Museveni's government. At the time of writing this book, Kahinda had a special role, as the chairman of the Pan-African movement all over the world. It is said that Rwigema was taken to Kenya, together with Mbabazi, who afterwards became minister for defence in 1974. When they met Museveni together, they crossed to Tanzania and went to Mozambique for training.

By 1979, many Banyarwanda had taken a second refugee to Kenya, for fear of Amin's state resaerch bureau. In Kenya, many worked as doctors and teachers. According to the UNHCR statistics, more than 15,000 Rwandans were registered as refugees in Kenya. They included former leaders of the UNAR, such as Michael Kayihura, John Rwangombwa, Gabriel Sebyeza, Augustin Mutabaruka, Francis Rubeka, Peter Mungarurire, Alexander Rutera, Joseph Micho and Kigeli who joined them from Uganda in 1979. These UNAR and other leaders had no political activities in Kenya apart from Gabriel Sebyeza who escaped death from Amin's prison.

THE BIRTH OF RANU

In 1979, a new political movement, known as the Rwandese Alliance National Unity (RANU), was formed by Rwandans, who had taken refuge in Kenya. Some writers have said that the alliance was formed in Uganda then changed its name from RRWF or Rwanda Refugees

Welfare Foundation, formed in June 1979, to help Rwandan refugees who had become victim of Amin's repression. This information was not true: I was informed by reliable sources that the general historical conditions were the very cause of RANU's formation. Many Rwandan liberation movements had been formed in exile since 1960. They had failed to make a successful revolution because of the lack of external conditions that was not in their favour.

Personally, I think that it is hard to get political organisers on a high level of political and ideological consciousness, or few principled cadres as political initiators, who carry out day-to-day political work, to agitate and propagate the cause of the revolution. Without revolutionaries, without a revolutionary theory and a revolutionary vanguard, a revolution always fails. For example, some Rwandans in exile, living in Kenya in 1979, doubted the political vision of RANU founders. One of the historian members of RANU, however, told the author that RANU was an alliance of people with different ideologies. The birth of the alliance, the author learnt, came at the time when Ugandan leaders were organising their unity conference in Moshi, Tanzania, in order to launch a conventional war against the regime of Idi Amin Dada. After discussions with Ugandan delegations to the unity conference and making contacts to various embassies in Kenya, the alliance was formed. Its leadership's composition was as follows:

- The chairman: Sebyeza Gabriel
- The vice chairman: Mutimura Zeno
- The general secretary: Karugahe Anthony
- The secretary for finance: Mutabaruka Austin
- The secretary for international relations: Karugarama Tarcisse
- The organising secretary or secretary for mobalisation: Kabanda Alloys
- The publicity secretary: Muzungu Munyaneza
- The secretary for youth: Rudasingwa Alphonse.

After its formation in early 1979, the alliance scored recognition by the Burundi government through the Burundi ambassador to Kenya. In fact, Mr Mukuli J acted as its patron. Its document was tabled at the Moshi unity conference, composed by Uganda political practical parties apposed to Idi Amin, and the conference saluted the stand taken by the people of Rwanda, against the most tyrannical and murderous regime in Africa. In July 1979, the alliance made an appeal to the O.A.U to put pressure on the regime in Rwanda to negotiate with Rwandan refugees outside of the country for their return.

In April 1979, when a combination of UNLA and TPDF forces took Kampala, RANU sent its secretary for international relations, Mr Karugarama, who was then a law student at Makerere University, to open a branch in Uganda. The branch was immediately formed with the following as members of the committee:

- Mr Patrick Mazimpaka: the chairman
- Mr Karamaga. R: the vice chairman
- Mr Joseph Mudaheranwa: the secretary

Other members of the branch committee included:

- Mr Peter Bayingana
- Mr Frank Mugambage
- Mr Focas Ntayombya
- Mr Haje Gashegu
- Miss Mukabaranga Beatrice

As a working strategy, some welfare and cultural associations were formed, including the Intercultural Association in Kenya. The Uganda National Liberation Army was composed of FRONASA of Yoweri Museveni, as the largest armed group. One of the FRONASA commanders was Fred Rwigema, a Rwandan refugee from Kahunge refugee settlement, who had joined FRONASA in 1979 in Mozambique.

Rwigema came into contact with LANU in 1979. He was introduced to its members in a meeting, at Mr Gashegu's home, by Mr Gabriel Sebyeza. In its first meeting in Nairobi, in August 1979, RANU vowed to wage struggle at all fronts, against the puppet regime of Habyarimana to Kenya and organised a solidarity party for the members, assuring the alliance of the Burundi's support. In the same year, a multitude of social organisations and cultural associations existed in different parts of the world. They included:

- The Impuruza group of Sacramento in Califonia, USA, with members in Washington DC, Los Angeles, New York and other cities.

- The Burundi groups. L'association des immigrees Rwandaise du Quebec, in Canada. The Rwandese Canadian Cultural Association in Ontario. The Isangano, combining all association in Belgium. The Abadaha, grouping all associations in Germany.

- The Congo Nile group of Zair. Groups in Tanzania with their newspaper *Ukoloni Mamboleo*

- The Abatabazi group of Cairo, grouping all the associations in North and West Africa. Other associations were found in Scandinavian countries, and African countries such as Senegal, Congo-Brazzaville, and Togo.

Even before RANU's formation, many student associations existed. The most remarkable union was A.G.E.R (Association General des Etudiants) Rwanda, based in Europe, and in the former USSR. The association was remarkable because it had members in Rwanda. Some of its leaders, like Seth Sendashonga, had relationships with RANU, as early as 1979.

Some political observers said that all those associations were formed by refugees, and that they lacked a revolutionary base. However, I dismiss this argument because a subjective initiative can be taken by any group of a society, irrespective of where it is based, as the essence of a revolution is the vision.

In 1980, Alex Kanyarengwe, Theoneste Lizinde, Donat Murego and company, organised a group against Habyarimana. They were not aimed at a new political horizon of the society, but a sectarian coup of the Ruhengeri clique, against the Gisenyi clique. The two groups had one political agenda: the Tutsi as the principal enemy. On the other hand, RANU had on agenda of returning the refugees to Rwanda. In a conversation with a historical RANU member, I learnt that some members of RANU were viewing the alliance as a coalition of force that could be brought together in order to liberate Rwanda. They had a vision of changing the entire society. That is why they have included Hutu in their high ranking.

When the Habyarimana regime was threatened by the confrontation between the Gisenyi and the Ruhengeri cliques, and that of Habyarimana's close associates, and his wife's powerful relatives, the RANU alliance had embarked on a massive recruitment campaign, not only in Uganda where it had shifted its operational base from Kenya, but in Burundi and Tanzania as well. It is even said that some RANU leaders had a discussion with Milton Obote before the 1980 elections, which brought him back to power. Obote, according to the same source, promised to support the alliance, claiming that he was an experienced Pan-Africanist, who understood the concern of Rwandan refugees. But Yoweri Museveni, the leader of FRONASA, had vowed to fight any leader who would interfere. FRONASA had qualitatively and quantitatively grown from strength, during Museveni's tenure of the Defence Ministry. He had created an invincible group of young cadres. Paul Kagame, who later became president of Rwanda, had joined FRONASA when UNLF overthrew Idi Amin. Sources told me that he was recruited to FRONASA by Fred Gisa Rwigema, his friend from the early childhood in the Kahunge settlement, where they lived together and studied at Rwengoro primary school. Sources said that Kagame was immediately sent to the African village in Cuba, for ideological and military training, with many other young FRONASA cadres.

When the group came back from Cuba, Museveni had finalised his plans to wage a second or a third struggle. Paul Kagame and his friend, Fred Rwigema, were among the twenty-seven fighters who launched a five-year war against the second Obote's regime, on February 6th 1981. It said that Habyarimana's security agent made several attempts to kill Fred Rwigema in the Ruwero Triangle. In 1982, the National Resistance Army of Yoweri Museveni had become stronger than a combination of the Tanzania army and Obote's army. Obote started making contradictory allegations that Museveni was a Munyarwanda and that Ugandans should all take up arms against Banyarwanda. In 1970, the same Museveni was Obote's principal secretary, a position he held up to the time of taking refuge to Tanzania when Idi Amini outed Obote in 1971.

Museveni is purely Munyankole of Bahima pastoral caste. The allegation that he was a Munyarwanda, a foreigner middling in the internal politics of Uganda, was totally baseless. There is, however, a social reality. The Banyankole, from western Uganda, are a community quite similar to the Rwandan social castes of Bahutu and Batutsi. The Bahima of Ankole, like the Batutsi of Rwanda-Burundi, are of the pastorist group, while the Bairu are cultivators like the Bahutu of Rwanda-Burundi. Some of Bairu of Ankole who had no political vision, exploited Obote's confusion and forced all Banyarwanda to go back to Rwanda, including not only Ugandan Banyarwanda, but many Bakiga of Kigezi, who had become victims of eviction of Banyarwanda. Many people were killed. It is said that between 30,000 and 50,000 Banyarwanda were killed in the districts of Ankole and about 65,000 heads of cattle were stolen by local authorities and the UPC youth. By December 1983, 40,000 Rwandans had crossed to Rwanda. Some Banyarwanda were killed and others were put in camps in Akagera national park. Those evicted from Lakai and Masaka districts took refuge in Tanzania. This made many young Tusti rebel and join those who fought the Ugandan government. In the years of

1982 and 1983, many young Banyarwanda joined Museveni's National Resistance Army, including most members of RANU. People like Alphonse Furam, who was a secondary school teacher in Kenya, Peter Baingana, who was a medical doctor in Mombasa's coast hospital and others, joined the NRA at the end of 1983. By 1984, the number of Banyarwanda fighters in the NRA was estimated at 6,000 guerrillas.

In other countries, RANU and other movements continued mobilisation and discussing principles governing genuine revolutions. Theogene Rudasingwa, then a student of medicine at Makerere University in Uganda, and a number of teachers and students in Kenya, had studied and discussed their programmes. They were believers of Chairman Mao of China. Mao taught that no revolution can be genuine without a revolutionary theory, and that a revolutionary movement must be formed based on, and guided by, that theory. Furthermore he believed that revolutionaries must embark on practice, only when they have become accomplished.

RANU's formation shows how it was totally lacking principle leaders, to act as its vanguard. Only a revolutionary movement, the group asserted, could lure people together, and to train carders, to agitate and politicise the people, in order to propagate their cause. It said that after that, RANU had united all Banyarwanda in Diaspora, without a visionary leadership, to champion the cause of the Rwanda people, rather than advancing the right of Rwanda refugees to return home. From 1979 to 1986, RANU was operating from Kenya where its central committee was based, its founder and first chairman, Mr Sebyeza had gone to Congo-Brazzaville, and later to Tanzania. Mr Mutimura Zeno acted as its chairman. The victory of Yoweri Museveni's NRA, was a victory for Banyarwanda and RANU, in particular. From 1986, RANU shifted from Kenya to Uganda, where it could work openly. When NRA stormed Kampala on January 26th 1986, Rwigema's army consisted of between 14,000 and 20,000 fighters. The NRA was numbering between 80,000 and 100,000 guerrillas. In 1987, at its general congress, RANU changed its name to a more militant front, the Rwanda Patriotic Front. Major Peter Bayingana took the leadership of RPF.

RANU BECOME R P F

In 1988, a congress of groups operating all over the world was held in Washington DC and resolutions were passed that refugees had the right to use any means to regain their fundamental birth rights. Professor Alexander Kimenyi was entrusted with the responsibility of coordinating the activities of all refugees, in the Diaspora. His group was Impuruza. In the RPF camp, it was only Bayingana who was active in the front, while other senior army officers, like Major General Fred Gisa Rwigema, Major Paul Kagame, Coloner Waswa, Major Kaka and many others had refused to join RPF. Major Baingana had been dismissed from his post as the director of medical services, and decided to lead the front. It is said that other senior army officers were opposed to Bayingana's leadership and wanted General Rwigema. Commander Musitu, who was in charge of training, was a supporter of Fred Rwigema, and had used his post to train many young Rwandans. Rwigema had become the de facto leader of Rwandans in Uganda. When Yoweri Museveni bestowed ranks on his top commanders, Rwigema was among the four of the first rank. He was given the rank of major general, and made a deputy minister of defence, assisting Museveni in the most important ministry in the country! Rwigema was made a general in the presence of Habyarimana.

Habyarimana, president of Rwanda at the time, was invited and taken to the Ruwero Triangle, to be shown the field of larger-scale human extermination by the UNRA of Milton Obote and General Tito Okello. He was accompanied to the killing field by General Rwigema. It was not a shocking and awful experience for Habyarimana, for in 1959 about half a million people were killed by the Belgian army, in collaboration with Habyarimana and Kayibanda. In 1987, Habyarimana made a statement that he and others crashed the Rwandan kingdom in 1960. Sources close to Rwigema said that the Ruwero visit by Habyarimana was a direct warning to him, that he would become more terrible than a tiger. When he returned to Kampala he said that no Rwandan who had been a refugee for over thirty years could claim Rwandan nationality. He said Rwandans, in various countries, should remain where they had been for years and Rwanda would help them to claim their nationalities to the countries that gave them a refugee status.

Habyarimana's visit to Uganda was followed by President Mitterand's son and wife's visit. Fred Rwigema took them to refugee settlements. Commenting on Rwigema's identification with his future enemies, people said that Museveni's intention was to show them the near future leaders of Rwanda. Both Habyarimana and the Mitterrands were invited by the new Museven's government, to discuss Banyarwanda refugees' political situation. It must be remembered that Habyarimana's security agents had tried to kill Rwigema, when he was still fighting the bush war in Uganda. He had even conspired with Obote to capture Museveni, when he passed through Rwanda.

In the RPF itself, bitter antagonism had developed between Bayingana and his group, and Rwigema had declined to be recruited by Bayingana into the RPF. He had his own armed group that included Major Paul Kagame. He had also made an alliance with a group of students from Makerere University in Uganda. The group was led by Dr Rudasingwa Theogene, who was then studying medicine. Rudasingwa's group was a revolutionary group of a few principled students. The group had a branch in Kenya. It was not a front or a movement, but a dissension group, studying the revolutionary theory. The group later met at Makerere University, under the chairman of Dr Rudasingwa. The group resolved that they had acquired a revolutionary concept of changing the situation based on a social revolution, but not merely on liberation. The group decided to organise itself into a vanguard party.

A front for national liberation was formed: Front De La Liberation Nationale (FROLINA). Before embarking on training its cadres as professional revolutionaries, the RPF became extremely hostile to the group, to the extent of planning to kill some of its members. The group decided to postpone its political work because of those threats. It was said that RPF feared the creation of many liberation movements because it lacked a clear-headed leadership. Any group that could be in the process of formation was termed *Igipinga*; a Kiswahili term, meaning a barrier. The RPF leaders did not accept any competition. The leaders had warned not to attempt to form political groups, which was a wise idea; if they divided themselves at that very early stage, it would not have been easy to reach their goal of rescuing their country. Professor Kimenyi, leader of the Impuruza group, had already been warned about his attempting to become a leader of Banywarwanda, only in the Diaspora (his group's activities).

In the meantime, the struggle for leadership in the RPF intensified. Major Bayingana had assumed the leadership of the front, without being elected by the congress. Sources close to the RPF leadership disclosed that Tito Rutaremara and Zeno Mutimura were opposed to Baingana's leadership, and as a result, Zeno was sacked from the central committee of the front and he went back to Kenya, while Rutaremara's coordination role was reduced to a mere spokesman of the front.

The conflict within the leadership became so alarming that Fred Rwigema decided to intervene. In an emergency meeting, in Kampala, in 1988, General Rwigema, supported by the armed group, decided to act as the RPF chairman, without neither being elected by the delegates, a member of the front's leaders. In the meeting, Rwigema warned that any so-called leaders, acting as an agent of divisionism, would not be tolerated. He appointed Major Paul Kagame and Dr Baingana to act as his vice-chairman. But for Dr Peter Baingana, the move was a terrible blow to his leadership and the move was totally unacceptable to him.

Bayingana's loss of RPF leadership divided the front into a few followers of Baingana, especially his former schoolmates, and the majority of followers of Gen Rwigema. In 1989, Baingana and his friends, in the RPF, organised a group of junior soldiers of about 300-

armed men. They were taken to the Akagera national park in Rwanda, by the Baingana group, to act as a source of the guerrilla war. When the Ugandan External Intelligence (ESO) learnt about the infiltration into Rwanda, by the Baingana group, Gen Rwigema was informed of the plan. Baingana was summoned to the NRA's high command for explanation. Baingana was not a member of the NRA's high commander or of its army council. He had been dismissed from the department of medical services due to the theft of drugs and equipment. At his wedding in 1989, General Mugisha-Muntu said that Baingana's services at the NR's sickbay during the bush war, overshadowed his theft in the department of medical services. He said that after weighing up the two, the statement added to Baingana's inability to be a leader. Apart from being an accomplished revolutionary, a leader must be a person of integrity.

It is said that when Baingana totally denied sending the young men to Rwanda, the NRA's High Command called General Rwigema from Northern Uganda, where he was fighting the Alice Lakwena's rebellion against the NRA. General Rwigema went to the Akagera and took back the armed young men to Uganda. It is said that they had spent three weeks in the Habyarimana's security service. When interviewed by some members of the ESO, and by General Rwigema himself, the young men disclosed that they were sent to Rwanda by a certain Charles Kabanda, who was Baingana's agent. Kabanda was arrested and detained but he refused to implicate Baingana in the invasion.

Sources close to the RPF said that it was then that General Rwigema decided to appoint Colonel Alex Kanyarengwe, who had been in Tanzania since his failed coup against Habyarimana in 1980. He was brought to Uganda by Rwigema, a factor that contributed to Baingana's fear of the front. After being side-lined from the leadership, Baingana travelled to a number of countries, like Canada, the USA, Europe, Burundi, Zaire, etc, consulting Rwandans and crusading against his friend Rwigema. It is said that in a meeting with some Rwandans in Bujumbura, Baingana had called Rwigema an illiterate so-called general! This language enraged General Salim Saleh, who, with General

Rwigema, had abandoned their secondary education to go to Mozambique, for military training.

Had it not been Museveni's intervention, Banyarwanda had to go to prison, sources said. When Baingana found that he was in trouble, he applied to join military training in the Nakasongola military academy in 1990. His application was approved by General Salim himself.

1990 was a historic year because it was the time when Fred Gisa Rwigema prepared a guerrilla war against the Habyarimana's regime. It was the year when Mr Pasteur Bizimungu and Varens Kajeguhakwa fled Rwanda to join the RPF. In 1990, Habyarimana requested the Ugandan government that a joint committee be created, to look into the problem of Rwandan refugees in Uganda or the problems of Rwandans immigrants in Uganda. UN commission *speciale sur les problemes des emigres* Rwandans.

Not a refugee had been set up by the Kigali regime, earlier in February 1989. The arrangement for the return of some refugees to Rwanda was totally rejected by the leaders of both the refugees and RPF. In June 1990, France authorised Habyarimana to introduce a multi-party system, as a strategy of depriving the RPF of potential partners (allies). France had replaced Belgium as a tutelary power because of its military guarantees, which Belgium could not provide. Habyarimana had to follow the order of France without delay. Many parties were formed, but all with the same ideology. They were formed to weaken the support of RPF that had infiltrated the country.

It was in 1990, when Paul Kagame, a major in the NRA, was sent to the USA for advanced training in military, at Fort-Leavenworth. It is said that General Rwigema had made several visits to the USA for discussions with senior USA army officers. My research was not able to discover the main purpose of his repeated visits. When discussing the source of the power on leadership struggle within the RPF, I came across the following arguments:

That Fred Rwigema was trained by Yoweri Museveni both militarily and ideologically, so that in future, his vision of Pan-Africanism can be a reality.

That RPF revolution was a practical implementation of that vision, and nobody, therefore, could replace Rwigema for the leadership of the front. Another argument was that RPF started in 1979, when Rwigema was in the bush war against Obote.

That when NRA overthrew the Oboto – Okello regime, Rwigema was made both a minister of defence under Museveni and a deputy army commander and that he had, on several occasions, declined to join the RPF, and therefore, he was more of a Ugandan leader than he a Rwandan leader.

Other views were that Fred Gisa Rwigema had no education that could enable him to be leader of Rwanda. Furthermore he had only a military capacity without intellectual calibre. Some sources close to the RPF leadership believed that the above differences were the major of the conflict between the Baingana camp, made up intellectual members of the front and the Rwigema camp, made up of the NRA's Rwandan fighters and RPF members who were not supporters of Bayingana. It is said that Mr Patrick Mazimpaka and Joseph Mudaheranwa-Karemera were the closest advisors of Peter Bayingana. However, I am convinced that good leadership is not based on academic papers from universities, but rather on clear-headedness. The ideological clarity is the only criteria for revolutionary leaderships. It is a product of the study of a revolutionary theory, of discussions and consultations and of a revolutionary practice. General Rwigema had no papers from a university, but Rwandans with a revolutionary concept are of the view that General Rwigema had acquired all the prerequisite conditions necessary for leading a revolution. Bayingana, on the other hand, had all the opportunities to acquire the theory but he did not exploit the favourable conditions. They totally lacked both theoretical and practical abilities to lead a revolution.

THE OCTOBER REVOLUTION

To many Banyarwandas inside Rwanda, the 1st October 1990 was a foreign invasion as RPF (Rwandan Patriotic Front) was a gang of attackers from Uganda. As for many Rwandans in the diaspora, they thought that the October war was intended for returning the refugees to their ancestral land. But Rwandan political analysts said that the October civil war was a revolution and they said that revolution was a political process of struggling for and taking over state power, in order to establish new relations and that a revolution, very often, can turn out to be a liberation, when the relations within a country remain the same.

On Monday 1st October 1990, a group of armed young men opened fire on the soldiers guarding the Kagitumba border post of Rwanda, killing some whilst the remaining fled. Within a few minutes, other armed combatants, in the Ugandan Army fatigues, were crossing from Uganda to Rwanda. The war of liberation in Rwanda began. When the RPF launched its war of liberation, Presidents Museveni of Uganda and Habyarimana of Rwanda were both in the USA, attending a U.N.C.E.F conference. It is said that before going to New York for the conference, Museveni had discussed the RPF cause with Habyarima's minister and that he had advised General Rwigema to continue negotiations with the Habyariman's regime. It said that Rwigema crossed the Kagitumba border with an army of about 2,500 men and women officers, from lieutenant colonels and majors, to lower ranking officers. When the RPF started the struggle, Paul Kagame, a major in the intelligence of the NRA, was not among the rank and file that started the war. He was in the USA for a military course. Sources close to the RPF say that Major Kagame was the de facto vice chairman of the front, deputising his mentor General Rwigema.

According to the Habyarimana regime's propaganda, that he was invaded by Uganda, there were no Banyarwanda in the RPF. They were Ugandans calling themselves RPF trained by the Americans, as both the French and Habyarimana's government claimed. The answer was false judgement, because those who attacked were Rwandan's willing to go back home.

Paul Kagame went to the USA when he was a major, and other officials like Fred Gisa Rwigema, before him, were just sent there for familiarisation tours, and for consultations, but not for training.

Since 1986, members of the RPF all over the world have been raising a lot of money for the revolution. Cultural exhibitions internationally were organised wherever Rwandans of diaspora were living and huge sums of money were collected. It has to be remembered that Rwigema had been a guerrilla commander for many years. He was a deputy minister for defence, deputy army commander for the NRA and other responsibilities enabled him to gather arms for his revolution.

It is believed that RPF invaded Rwanda with large equipment such as heavy machine guns, motors, BM 21 multiple rocket-launchers, rifles, ZUG automatic cannons and many others arms. This was because they expected to fight a short war and they carried a limited amount of ammunition and weapons. The only reason is that the puppet regime of Rwanda could not resist visionaries and experienced fighters and they could not focus in any way in a short war. Calling the RPF an invading force is lacking an analysis of socio-political realities of Rwanda. Years of exile could not deprive Rwandan refugees of their basic and fundamental rights, as Rwandans they might have been helped morally and financially by other countries.

Years of French and Belgian puppet regimes in Rwanda, by visionary and experienced fighters, could not, in any way, have focussed in a short war.

Investigations carried out by the author revealed that RPF's top commanders knew very well the general historical conditions of their society. What mattered were the enemy forces. Admittedly, their geographical position had a number of disadvantages to the struggle. The RPF leaders knew that they had, first and foremost, to unite the people because colonialist and their agents, after the so-called independence, had divided the population into artificial races, terming Batutsi as foreigners and Bahutu as the real owners of the land. The expectation of a short war, therefore, was totally out of the question. The battle hardened and experienced RPF, guided by acquired revolutionary principles, could not have planned a short war. The political reality on the scene, on the 1st October 1990, was that Rwanda's war of liberation had begun.

GENERAL FRED GISA RWIGEMA

Commander Fred, as his comrades-in-arms were calling him, died on the 2nd of October 1990. Rwigema was a legend amongst Banyarwanda in Uganda and in some of other parts of the world. His long and distinguished military career, his revolutionary and Pan-African service in armed struggles and his achievement in the NRA, had caned him recognition even among many Ugandans. He was termed a charismatic commander. But who killed Commander Fred? The assassination of General Rwigema has been kept secret to-date! But insiders of the front's leadership knew, even before the outbreak of the armed struggle, that Commander Fred could be killed by his rivals. This is because he was too good and trusted everybody in his leadership. Therefore, people said that if he did not take maximum preventive measures he would be killed.

It is well known that, when Peter Bayingana was removed from the leadership of the front, he and his close accomplices started their vicious plans to eliminate him. Speculative guesses were aired by both the Habyarimana regime, Banyarwanda in Uganda and even the Rwandan Patriotic Army. The first speculation was that Rwigema was killed by one of the frequent hazards of war. That he was standing on a small hill, watching Habyarimana's soldiers fleeing, when one of the fleeing soldiers turned around and killed him with a single shot. This guess was not convincing. In his statement after Rwigema's death, Habyarimana himself denied the assassination, but said that Rwigema had been wounded by his soldiers and that he had been taken to America for treatment. This statement was made after his return from the UNCF conference.

Another guess is that Commander Fred was assassinated by Bayingana and his group who had been planning to kill him because of his popular support among the RPA and Banyarwanda in general. It is said that his death was immediately reported to his comrades, in Uganda, by one of his bodyguards, who fled to Uganda after the assassination. The NRA's high command warned the RPF not to comment on Rwigema's death. A Ugandan journalist, Mr Sezicyeye, said that he visited the RPF on the 5th October and found that Major Bayingana was very much in charge of the RPF. Other statements include stepping on a land mine. It was obvious that Rwigema's assassination was a big blow to his RPF. Habyarimana's army took the advantage to recapture the Gabrio camp in the Umutara province, after the French troops had come to their rescue. Confronted by French, Belgian and Zaire troops, who had come to rescue their Habyarima, the RPF tactically retreated to Uganda, on the order of President Museveni, it was claimed. Rumours had it that President Museveni sent General Salim-Saleh with a group of commanders, to arrest Bayingana and his accomplices. They were taken to the Mbarara military barracks and tried by the NRA's court martial this took place before the withdrawal of the RPF, the rumour asserted.

The French Embassy in Kampala said that Bayingana and his friend Bunyenyezi, were tried by the RPF court and killed on the orders of Major Paul Kagame. People have dismissed this speculative rumour saying that Major Kagame was still in the USA, when Rwigema's killers were tried. It is said that after Bayingana and his accomplice's death, Major Paul Kagame was called back from USA after only three and half months of his two years course duration. He was appointed the RPF commander by President Museveni and introduced to RPF troops by General Salim-Saleh who was then NRA factor commander.

Returning from the UNCEF conference in New York where he was with Habyarimana, Museveni said that he had warned Habyarimana that he had no alternative but to negotiate with RPF because it was a formidable force that could not be defeated on the battle front! This statement revealed that Museveni knew of the plan. After all, Rwigema was his close comrade. He had trained him in

Tanzania, fought Idi Amini together, and started the Ruwero Triangle struggle together. The RPF organised and mobilised members openly and funds were raised at Rugogo National Stadium and at other public places. Habyarimana knew of the impending revolution, but chose to ignore all the warnings. He had made it clear that he would not accept to negotiate with the refugees and that after thirty years in exile, nobody could claim to be a refugee. In addition Rwanda was too overpopulated. It is also said that Habyarimana had an assurance from France that the attack by the RPF from Uganda would not be tolerated by France, and that it would be the end of President Museveni's rule in Uganda. It meant that France and Belgium had made decisions to invade Uganda, therefore would the RPF launch its attack against the Habyarimana regime from Uganda. Habyarimana counted on France and Belgium's backing in any event, and he was very right!

THE SECOND PHASE OF THE WAR

By the end of October 1990, the RPA had completely withdrawn from the Akagera National Park, after heavy losses, due to the confusion caused by the death of its leader. In fact, on the 30th October, the Habyarimana regime announced the end of the war, and celebrations of the victory and death of Rwigema were held throughout the country. The RPF's second phase of the war started in Byumba Province, when a surprise attack at the Rwanda–Uganda border of Uganda Gatuna, led by Commander Twahirwa known as "Dodo", killed and maimed soldiers who were celebrating the victory. The protracted war had begun.

In Paris, Jean Christophe Miterand, the president's son of France at the time, who was in charge of the foreign office, gave an assurance to Habyarimana that French troops would finish the invaders, within two or three months. Troops were sent from the Central African Republic, and Belgium sent a battalion to Kigali. A special division of about 5,000 troops were sent by Mobutu president of Zaire at the time, and immediately went into action. In order to draw the French and Belgian troops into action like Mobutu's troops, the regime of Habyarimana staged a fake attack on Kigali, on 5th October 1990, from 1am to 7am. Within a few days, France had increased its troops to more than 600 men. The French vowed to crush the RPF in order to protect their intermediary. In addition France was very bitter about the English status of the RPF leadership. It was said that anybody speaking English thought that the Anglo-Saxon people stole Canada and India from the French. They also exiled Napoleon and burnt Jeanne d'Arc alive. It is said that the French considered President Museveni to be an Anglo-Saxon because he was a big threat to the French interests. Happy with the French support, Habyarimana declared that he was ready to talk with what he termed the invaders, on condition that they left the soil of Rwanda and that he would not talk with the RPF, but with forces backing them. He meant Uganda.

As for the Belgians, the job of finishing the RPF was left to the French, because they had gained more from the Habyarimana's tenure of office, and were more advanced than them. Belgium retained a limited number of troops in the capital, Kigali, claiming that they were kept there to protect its 1,700 nationals. Belgium's prime minister and its foreign minister travelled to Kenya where they met President Arap Moi of Kenya, to convince President Museveni not to support the RPF. On their return to Belgium, they asked France, the Netherlands and Germany to organise and transport an inter-African peace-keeping force to Rwanda. In Rwanda, claims of Tutsi feudalist's invasion were intensified. A massive wave of killings and arrests was launched. Even before the RPF attack, killings took place in Commune Murambi and in the Bugesera region. Many Batutsi were massacred. Tutsi women were raped before being killed, those taken prisoners were beaten to death, and the soldiers threatened to kill all the Batutsi, should the RPF attack Kigali. The minister of defence gave an order to kill all suspects. In the Kibulira Commine, more than 1,400 Tutsi civilians were massacred and their homes burned. The killings were an ideology of eliminating Bututsi, as it had been formulated and planned by Belgian Colonialists, and their Catholic Church.

Previously from the 1960s, a warning had been issued to exiled refugees that if any attempt to attack the regime of Kayibanda was made, all Batutsi remaining in Rwanda would be eliminated. The same warning was repeated in 1990 when the RPF launched the war of liberation, the ideology was tested and a conclusion was reached in 1994. When Habyarimana out sided Kayibanda, France replaced Belgium in the political orientation of Rwanda, and Belgium played a subsidiary role in politics, but remained the financial and economic masters of the country. Some Rwandans were of the view that France became the master of affairs because of the language factor. Others thought that the supervision of Rwanda was purely ideological.

THE FRENCH LINK

On Friday October 6th 1990, the French prime minister, Michel Rocard, declared on French TV, on the *TF1* channel, that they had sent troops to Rwanda to protect their citizens. The troops, from then, supervised the operations of the army; they manned roadblocks and armed the army, known as FAR or Rwanda's Armed Forces. They had vowed to crush the R.P.F within a short period of time. Their perception of the war was that they had to help Rwanda to crush an invading force of Museveni, an Anglo-Saxon agent! The French had a conviction that there had been a revolution in Rwanda in 1959, similar to the 1789 French revolution that had a legitimate content. The aristocrat had been chased from power. The French claimed that the Hutu regime in Rwanda was democratic because it represented 85% of the total population of Rwanda. France made contacts with Egypt and South Africa for arms supplied to Habyarimana. Habyarimana's army increased from 5,200 in 1990 to 50,000 in 1992.

We can talk about genuine liberation but no comparison can be made between the 1959 killings of Batutsi in Rwanda by the colonial administration, because of the independence crisis and the 1789 bourgeois revolution in France that reformed feudalism. It said that, to completely crush patriotic forces, that wanted to solve a national question, Belgians had to massacre the people, in order to establish a satellite government of local shopkeepers. Nothing like a revolution took place, because a revolution is a violent or non-violent change, by liberating the people from exploitation and oppression, in order to establish a new democratic process.

In a colony, the principal enemy is colonialism and in a neo-colony the principal and primary enemy is the international bourgeoisie with their few local compradors. We cannot, therefore, talk about the 1960 revolution in Rwanda when the country was undergoing a decolonisation process. We cannot talk about the aristocrats being chased from power in Rwanda, when the country was still ruled by colonialists and we cannot talk about the Hutu majority, because Rwanda had no classes before the invasion of colonialism. Rwanda had only castes based on different means of survival.

We can talk about Rwanda as a neo-colony of France by the time of the R.P.F's war of liberation. We cannot talk about Museveni's invading Francophone forces, but we can talk about a Pan-African initiative to fight an agent clique struggle, waged by real sons and daughters of the land, in order to get rid of one of Africa's actioners.

THE MULTI-PARTY POLITICS

Democracy can be viewed by political analysts on the basis of their ideological perceptions. But they all agree that it has to refer to the people. Abraham Lincoln said that it meant a "government of the people, and for the people". But he did not explain who the people were. Are they the haves or the downtrodden? Some analysts say that multi-parties are not a genuine democracy because it is not class-contraction-oriented. Its contradiction is not of a socio-economic category, but rather a mere power struggle, within the same class. The class used its economic power to win political power. The have-nots have no chance of standing for elections, and their only right is to caste votes for the rich, whichever party he comes from. The poor are taxed to finance the programmes benefiting the rich. In Rwanda, multi-party politics was imposed on the people in 1959, with the aim of weakening the popular struggle for independence. It is said that more than twenty parties were created. The direct outcome was the first genocide of 1959, termed the most systematic human massacre. The second multi-party democracy was established in 1991, on the orders of France in order to bar people from supporting the RPF. Habyarimana's MRND or Mouvement Révolutionnaire National Pour le Développement, had been the sole party in the country.

Many new parties such as the following were created: the MDR or Mouvement Democratique Republicain, an anti-Tutsi so-called movement which became a tool of Belgium to exterminate the Tutsi in 1959. The party was led by Faustin Twagiramungu, Kayibanda's son-in-law. The PSD, or Parti Social Democrate, created in May 1991, under the leadership of Frederic Nzamurambaho. He once said that the 1990 war was a conflict between the majority Hutu and the minority Tutsi. The PL, or Party Liberal, with a liberal tendency on the Hutu ideology.

According to Batutsi who were in Rwanda at the time, they liked the party, thinking that its leaders were ready to accommodate them. But like MRD and PSD, the Liberal Party was a sectarian formation, as later proved by its leaders, like Justin Mugenzi. The PDC, or Parti Democrate-Chretien,was led by Nayinzira Jean-Nepomuceni, who thought that he could attract the support of the Catholic Church. But the church was an action and serious partner of Habyarimana's MRND through its head, Mgr Thaddee Nsengiyumva. The primate of Rwanda and his mentor, Mgr Andre Perraudin, were leading architects of the Hutu ideology, that exterminated Bututsi in 1994 and before. Nevertheless the Catholic Church supervised PDC's political operations. In November 1991, the church and Belgian Christian parties declared a pro-Hutu common stand. The meeting in Belgium was attended by Palipehutu, or *parti pour la leberation du peuple* Hutu of

Burundi, and later Palipehutu carried out terrorist attacks in Burundi. In order to make the French more satisfied, Habyarimana allowed the formation of other political organisations, such as the PSP or Rwandan Socialist Party.

Partie Socialiste Rwandais was led by a Tutsi medical doctor, Mr Rutijana from Patrice Lumumba University in Mosco, USSR. Because the party was led by a Tutsi, very few Batutsi dared to join it. Their fear was understandable.

In 1992, a special movement was set up by Habyarimana, with a mission of defending the republic. The party, known as CDR, or the Coalition for the Defence of the Republic, was headed by Jean Shyirambere Barahinyura. Writers of the history of Rwanda in the 1990s say that this party was formed by racist Hutu radicals. Barahinyura had written a book about the tyrannical nature of the Habyarimana regime. It is said that his wife had been in prison for six years because of being involved in the Lizinde and Kanyarengwe 1980 coup.

When Barahinyura learnt that Alex Kanyarengwe was the RPF chairman, he joined it later in 1990. He left the RPF, accusing it of being a Tutsi-dominated front and went back to Rwanda, where together with a number of associates like Jean-Bosco Barayagwiza and Martin Bucyana, he formed CDR. Defending the republic meant that the RPF was fighting to institute a kingdom in Rwanda that had been crushed by republicans. MDR was also said to be a republican party. However, to revisit our argument, feudalism, or rather the kingship, in Rwanda had been relegated to the museum of history because its material foundation was completely destroyed by colonialism.

The 1780 industrial revolution, in Europe, negated feudal rule and was replaced with a new bourgeois mode. It is therefore, not only an ideological myopia but also an utter bankruptcy of understanding the progressive development of humanity in general, and of Rwanda in particular. Suffice to say that the Hutu ideology, as some writers have termed the divide and rule strategy in Rwanda, entailed sectarian tactics of turning the people one against the other, while the enemy watched from the pedestal. This was the mission of CDR and the associate organisations.

On the war front, the RPF had already taken control of almost the whole of Byumba prefecture or province, some communes or districts of the Ruhengeri province and areas of the Umutara, by the beginning of 1992. In January 1991, the RPF's overrunning of Ruhengeri military fortress became an eye-opener to the French, that the front was becoming an invincible force. During the operation, Colonel Lizinde was another follower prisoner who was set free. Lizinde was another front-line cadre of the Hutu ideology. He had published a book to this effect. Ruhengeri town was occupied by the RPF for a day and then withdrew to their area of operation. Lizinde, Biseruka and a number of other prisoners chose to join the RPF. Those who refused to join the front were allowed to go to their homes but were later arrested by the Habyarimana's army. Earlier, Colonel Uwihoreye, who was in charge of the Ruhengeri prison, was ordered to kill all the prisoners, but he refused to obey orders from Kigali. He was later arrested and jailed for a year, and when temporarily released, he took refuge to Belgium. Asked about his release, Colonel Lizinde said that it was God's will that he was free. He mentioned no word of thanks to RPF. But for the RPF, what mattered was a large amount of military equipment and ammunition they got from the army garrison, and the political victory they once more scored. To the Habyarimana regime and their masters, the message was that the front had the capacity to win the war. The political and psychological victory of the RPF in Ruhengeri became a factor of mobilisation. Many young men and women joined the front from Rwanda itself, from as far as Canada and Europe. The front had already trained cadres from Tanzania, Burundi, Uganda and Zaire.

In normal revolutionary struggles, the front-line leadership must be supported by civilians. In Rwanda, however, the general conditions, especially the socio-political leadership of the front, eradicate mythical complexes. After realising that the Patriotic Army was becoming an invincible force, and that it was getting popular support in the liberated areas of Byumba, Habyarimana and his mentors thought that moving people from the contested areas, could be a strategy to isolate the RPF.

It said that local Hutu were running away from the RPF, contrary to liberation processes. It is said that about 300,000 people had run away from the RPA advance by January 1991, from the Byumba areas of operation. However, the reality remains that whenever the RPF was harassing the Habyarimana Army, the civilians were paying the price.

The Hutu had to be displaced to deprive the RPA of their support, and of making ideological gains. The Tutsis, on the other hand, had to be eliminated, even in areas where the army was controlling. When the RPA over-ran and occupied the town of Ruhengeri on 27th January 1991, a wave of massacres was carried out, in the Bigogwe area of Kisenyi and in Gaseke and Kinigi communes of Ruhengeri, far from the town itself. The Hutu ideology was that all Bututsi had to be exterminated.

The Bagogwe were Tutsi peasants in the Kisenyi Province. Another massacre of the Tutsi took place in the Bugesera area near Burundi, far from the Byumba Province, where the front was carrying out its mobile operations. A political scientist from Uganda, Professor Mahmood Mamdani, writing on the RPF's war of liberation said that, instead of liberating the masses, the front liberated mountains. He meant that civilians were running away from their liberators. It is my view that such analysis is not going down to the heart of the problem. In a situation like that of Rwanda, in which contradictions were complex, the essence is to target the civilians displaced by the Habyaramina army, at gun point, as the RPF was advancing. Few civilians, who managed to escape the army of Habyaramina, were living happily in the liberated zone of the RPF.

PEACE NEGOTIATION

In March 1991, a Zairean-sponsored ceasefire agreement was signed, between RPF and FAR, in N'sele near Kinshasa, after realising that the

RPF was routing the FAR at every encounter. Habyarimana asked his close friend, Mobutu of Zaire, to negotiate the ceasefire on his behalf. Mobutu pretended to act as a mediator, but in vain. The RPF multiplied its attacks, contrary to the arrangements. The Gatuna road to Uganda remained closed. From 1990 to the time of ceasefire negotiations, Tutsi were being killed in every part of the country.

Some observers said that the killings were prompted by attempts to prevent political parties from supporting or sympathising with the RPF. It was intended to sabotage the process of democratisation. Many didn't accept these views. It indicated that multi-parties were not democratic, because they are an anti-people process, not for the people.

The sharing of cabinet posts in April, between MRND and internal parties, was one of Habyarimana's tactics to unite the Hutu according to his ideology, against the RPF. The MRND took nine posts, MDR took five ministries and the rest of the parties had one ministry.

It is said that the multi-party government, of Dr Nsengiyaremye Dismas, tried to abolish the policy of equilibrium in education and employment, but Habyarimana resisted the reform. Equilibrium meant that Tutsi in education and employment had to remain 15% as per their national statistics But Rwandans both in and outside the country questioned the coalition government. They wondered whether it was truly democratic or a mere cosmetic change. In form, it was a multi-party government, but in the real sense, that government was a product of the French machination in order to help Habyarimana to maintain Hutu solidarity. When Gapyisi Emmanuel and his friends in the MDR initiated what they termed d'initiative paix et democratie, as a reconciliation initiative, its aim was to warn and educate Hutu, in the coalition. We have exposed the colonial gimmicks behind this revolution.

Eighteen months after the arrival of more French troops to protect the regime, their mission in Rwanda lay open by the refusal of the French ambassador to join a delegation of the USA, Canada and other OECD countries in order to meet President Habyarimana and express their concern about the continued wave of killings of Tutsi, in the country in general, and in the Bugesera region in particular. It was said that the

French considered the USA and Canada complaint about the killings to be a plot by the Anglo-Saxons. Instead of telling Habyarimana to stop the massacres, the French multiplied the supply of weapons and ammunitions by about $12 million. Lieutenant Colonel Chollet had been entrusted with the overall command of the operations against the Rwandan Patriotic Army, RPF. Later, the command of FAR was given to Lieutenant-Colonel Maurin, according to a French paper, *La Liberation* of June 1992. Even the French minister for cooperation had to come to see how the operation was being carried out, in March 1992.

On the government's side, the minister for international cooperation, Mr Ngulinzira Boniface, met and discussed with Mazimpaka of the RPF about peace and ceasefire. On 6th June 1992, a delegation of political parties like MDR, PSD and PL met with RPF's delegation that included Dr Rudasingwa Theogene, Mr Mazimpaka Patrick and Dr Bihozagara Jacques, in Brussels for discussions. On 4th July, a ceasefire was signed, and the RPF announced the end of the armed struggle, but that it had to resort to political negotiations. In the Paris negotiations, the RPF managed to convince the French that the negotiations should be continued in Africa, and that Arusha in Tanzania was its ideal choice. The French and their Kigali lackeys finally accepted Arusha. It has to be remembered that Arusha had been a centre of African liberation. It was therefore a political victory for the front, to take the regime of Habyarimana to Arusha as Habyarimana wanted Zaire or another French-speaking country.

THE ARUSHA PEACE TALKS

In July 1992 peace negotiations started in Arusha, Tanzania. The government delegation, at the negotiations, included Boniface Ngurinzira; minister of defence and Ambassador Kanyarushoke. The RPF negotiators included Pasteur Bizimungu, Dr Theogene Rudasingwa and Patrick Mazimpaka. Before reaching a compromise on some of the most important conditions, agents of the regime of Habyarimana organised demonstrations, in the prefectures of

Ruhengeri and Gisenyi. In areas of Kibuye, members of the Tutsi community were killed, as an indication of opposing the talks. Habyarimana told his followers that the team in Arusha was given instructions not to make any decisions without his approval. The people of Rwanda should have been able to rest assured that necessary precautions had been taken. The regime and the oppositions had vowed not to compromise what Hutu ideology calls the majority lure, brought by the 1959 social revolution.

On 18th August 1992, an agreement was signed between the government and the RPF. The negotiation was observed by many countries such as Tanzania, Uganda, France, Belgium, the USA, Canada and Germany. France opposed the invitation of Great Britain by the RPF. France alleged that the front was a creation of Museveni and the British.

Political analysts thought that that big powers came to supervise peace talks in Arusha because Habyarimana was one of the most reliable agents of capitalists. They said that, in addition, Tanzania was known for its leftist attitude, and that there was no way that Western countries could allow strategic Rwanda to fall to the left or to become a socialist country. Other views were that there existed international contradiction between France and Belgium, on one side, and USA and Britain on the other. I found that the two views are acceptable because of the principle of globalisation in the USA.

When the formation of a provisional government was agreed upon, on the 18th August 1992, CDR organised to meet Habyarimana and asked to fire Nsengiyaremye and his cabinet. CDR organised demonstrations against the way the peace process was being conducted. It thanked President Mitterrand and the French for supporting the Hutu cause. France had 1,100 troops fighting the RPF at the time and, before the agreement was signed, France sent 150 men to reinforce its force. Habyarimana's army were lead by the French, and they were training his new recruited men, in all training camps. All Interahamwe and Impuzamugambi (MRND and CDR) were being trained by the French Army in Rwanda.

France expressed its full support to CDR in a letter written to CDR's leader, Jean-Bosco Barayagwiza, for his support to the intervention force in Rwanda. CDR said that France was a saviour of Rwanda because it was fighting feudalist invaders. They condemned *Radio Rwanda*, and accused it of being an indirect agent of the RPF. In a meeting called by Barayagwiza, CDR leaders resolved to establish a newspaper known as *Kangura*, and to set up a radio station known as *RTLM* or *Radio and Television of the Thousand Hills*. Then newspaper *Kangura*, headed by Hassan Ngeze, started publishing the Ten Commandments of the old Parmehutu of Kayibanda, warning all Bahutu about Hutu ideology and about the achievements of the 1959 social revolution and the 1961 referendum. Jean-Peirre Chretien wrote about racist propaganda in Rwanda in 1991.

In June, Nsengiyaremye and Gasana attempted to reorganise the army (FAR) in their favour, and they managed to convince Habyarimana to retire as top army commander, including people such as Colonel Serubuga, Buregeya, Rwagafitira and Hakizimana. They were succeeded by Nsabimana, Gatsinzi and Ndindiliyimana. It meant that the first group hated Batutsi and were opposed to any compromise with the RPF. The group was termed extremist, but the commandments were taught to all Bahutu from the colonial epoch, to date. Even the new commandments had the same belief.

While peace talks continued in Arusha, a group of top advisors to Habyarimana were organising killer squads, known as the Zero Network. The squads were exposed by Belgians in Brussels. Professor Philip Reytit Jens and Senator Will Kupers, told the Belgian Senates that the death squad was created in Rwanda. They termed it the Zero Network; comparable to the Latin American death squad model. The squad had killed Batutsi in Bugesera. It was constituted by Habyarimana's brothers-in law and Colonel Sagatwa, his personal assistant. Colonel Bagosora of the ministry of defence was among the creators of the Zero Network.

When the Belgians disclosed the network, Habyarimana's government did not dismiss the allegations. The RPF knew the plan and issued a warning that, if the squad started massacring people once more, the RPF not only would start the war but it would be the end of the tyrannical regime. The warning created fear and panic among the army of Habyarimana and their French masters. They armed CDR and MRND militia. By late 1992, every plan had been accomplished; ready to exterminate all Batutsi and those Bahutu believed to be supporters of the RPF. Political parties in Habyarimana's government said that it was only a few extremists who were planning to kill Batutsi. However, I dismissed this extremist simplistic view. I think that the Tutsi extermination plan was made by Belgian colonisers because King Musinga and, later, his son Rudahigwa, were bitter about opposing the Belgian colonisation and the influence of the Catholic Church. The extermination of the Tutsi was not at all an outcome of contradictions between Tutsi and Hutu, but, rather, an antagonistic contradiction between colonialists and the people of Rwanda. This was through the supervisors of the colonial operations, known as the *umwami*, and colonial chiefs. The Hutu cause was nothing but a disguising strategy by the church and the colonial administration, in order to weaken a national resistance. Turning the victims one against the other is a well-known strategy in the divide and rule policy of colonialists.

As for the Arusha agreement, Habyarimana angrily declared that it was a mere draft, and that nobody was under obligation to adhere to it. December 1992 and January 1993 were marked by CDR and MRND demonstrations, against the agreement. On 22th November 1992, Leo Mugesera, who was the vice chairman of MRND in Gisenyi, addressed a meeting in Kabaya that the opposition parties had plotted with the Inyenzi or RPF, the enemy of Rwanda, to occupy the Byumba prefecture and to undermine the Rwandan army. He wondered why the plan was not put into effect. He said that they had made a big blunder in 1959 by allowing the Tutsi to go out and that a shortcut was the only way to send them back to Ethiopia, through the River Nyabarongo.

After Mugesera's declaration, the massacre of the Batutsi started in many regions of the country, and demonstrations against the power-sharing agreement were organised. In February 1993, the RPF decided to take military action against the FAR. Many military camps in the prefecture of Byumba were over-run by the RPF, causing the FAR to withdraw in disarray. The FAR forced more than 3,000,000 into camps, who had earlier been forced to leave their homes, to run away with them, so that they would not support the RPF. Writers on the politics of the time said that civilians were running away from their so-called liberators. This statement is false because, from the outbreak of the liberation war, civilians became a tool of the Hutu ideology. The FAR wanted the world to believe that it was a Hutu-Tutsi question, but not a political question. Some Hutu who managed to escape the FAR were very happy in the RPF liberated zones as I said. Claiming that the Hutu civilians were afraid of the RPF Tutsi feudalists, was an utter ignorance of Rwanda's politics.

In Rwanda, it has been repeated that Hutu-Tutsi castes were advanced by colonialisation. Nowhere in the world had primitive natural activities for survival, brought about antagonistic conflicts as often proposed in the history of Rwanda. Turning Hutu civilians against Tutsi civilians was not an accident of history, but a pure and simple colonial machination. Apart from overrunning fifty positions of the FAR and their French supporters, the RPF almost overruled Kigali, the capital. It was Colonel Alex Kanyarengwe, the RPF chairman, who announced a unilateral ceasefire from Byumba. I came to realise that there have been a number of reasons that made RPF stop the war.

First of all, RPF did not want to engage in a conventional war with the French army. France said that the offensive was an open provocation to its army, that such aggression was not tolerable. New troops were rushed to Rwanda and a massive quantity of ammunition was brought in.

Secondly, the RPF did not want the implementation of the Arusha agreement because it was advantaging Habyarimana and his colleagues (23rd February 1993). Marcel Debarge, the French minister for cooperation, arrived in Kigali, and ordered a unity between political opposition parties and Habyarimana's party against the RPF.

Immediately a meeting between MRND, CDR and ten minor parties was organised and unanimously resolved the following:

- The meeting condemned Uganda for starting the war in Rwanda.
- It recorded its appreciation to France for its military intervention.
- It condemned the RPF for trying to take power by force of arms.
- It called upon the army to fight the enemy with resolve.

Some members of the opposition parties were sent to Burundi, to meet the RPF delegation. The discussions lasted for a week and came up with the following resolutions, among many others:
- The renewal of peace talking in Arusha
- A durable ceasefire
- Unconditional withdrawal and repatriation of all foreign troops, including French.
- The immediate return of displaced civilians to their homes.
- The arrest and legal action against all those involved in the massacres of Rwandans in the country.

The RPF justified its offensive by saying that it had launched an attack in order to punish criminals who were killing the people. It also said that its attack was a warning to the negotiators of the government, not to sabotage the Arusha accord. But those who knew the front very well told me that RPF was a liberation movement that had brought together all forces that could be united, with the main objective of conquering state power by crushing imperialism and its local hangers-on.

The initiative of Habyarimana to unite all Hutu parties had been tried by Emanuel Gapyisi, a year later. Habyarimana's meeting was attended by Murego Donat who led the MDR delegation, by Stanislas Mbonampeka of the PL, by Paul Secyugu representing PSD, by Humuriza Gaspard, representing PDC and delegations from small parties. The meeting, however, was not supported by all who considered the RPF to be the principal enemy, although they opposed the leadership of Habyarimana. Those who refused to attend Habyarimana's unity meeting, had a plan of accommodating the RPF in their next democratic government, but did not envisage sharing power with the front. They had the same vision that Batutsi were a minority race that would in no way be allowed to lead the country. They included, Twagiramungu Faustin and Nsengiyaremye of MDR, Fredrick Nzamurambaho and Gatabazi of the PSD and Justin Mugenzi of PL, together with their supporters. The Twagiramungu-Nzamurambaho unity condemned the Gapyisi-Murego alliance, but Gapyisi had managed to create a broad anti-RPF, and anti- Habyarimana alliance. The movement had become so popular that it proved to be a threat, not only to Habyarimana, but to the opposition alliance as well. The RPF knew that all the factions were its enemies and it was ready to negotiate peace with any alliance.

On 18th May, Gapyisi was shot dead by unknown gunmen. Twagiramungu and the RPF were accused of planning his death. The popularity of Mr Gapyisi was a threat to Habyarimana's status quo and therefore, he had to be eliminated. After killing Gapyisi, Habyarimana turned to Nsengiyaremye. He accused the prime minister of conspiring with the RPF to oust him. On 6th July 1993, Nsengiyaremye wrote a letter to Habyarimana, accusing him of sabotaging the peace accord, and of preparing attacks on various politicians.

On 17th July 1993, President Habyarimana replaced Dr Nsengiyaremye with a woman from MDR party, who was minister of education. Mme Agathe Uwiringiyamana was mandated to sign another agreement of power sharing. But MDR, anti-Twagiramungu group of Murego and Karamira, protested at the appointment of Agathe to the post of prime minister, because she was in the camp of Twagiramungu. They appointed a Hutu power member in the name of Jean Kambanda. Hutu power was a support of Habyarimana, but because Habyarimana wanted to divide MDR further, he refused to replace Agathe with Kambanda.

In Arusha negotiations went on and the sharing of military leadership was a bitter issue of disagreement. Habyarima's army wanted a 40-60% ratio, with the RPF taking the 40% only. The front proposed

50% equal distribution of the whole new army. Close assistants of Habyarimana, such as his brothers-in-law and his top military aids, including Colonels Serubuga and Rwagafirita, totally disassociated themselves with the Arusha discussions, intending to share power with Batutsi. They said that they would, in no way tolerate the selling out of the country. On 4th August 1993, however, President Ali Hassan Mwinyi of Tanzania, who was the mediator of peace talks, decided to call a regional summit of heads of state and government, to Dares-Salaam, in order to look into the sabotage of the peace agreement. The following were called:

- President Yoweri Museveni of Uganda
- President Habyarimana of Rwanda
- President Melchior Ndadaye of Burundi
- President Ali Hassan Mwinyi himself
- Prime Minister Faustin Bilindwa of Zaire

The accord was again signed by the RPF and Habyarimana himself this time. The accord had all the previous provisions such as:

- The ceasefire agreement
- The formation of a transitional government
- The power-sharing modalities
- The form of repatriation or all refugees
- The agreement for integrating the new army
- The setting up of monitoring forces

Habyarimana had signed the agreement because his army and his French supporters had been completely defeated, both on the battlefield and at the round-table, by the patriotic front. On 31th August 1993, he went to Uganda to meet Museveni. But Museveni invited RPF to the meeting, and Habyarimana refused to meet the delegation. On 14th September, Habyarimana decided to go to Burundi to see the new president. He called for Hutu solidarities, but Burundi was not favouring such solidarity and the meeting was indecisive. When Ndadaye was put in power, Habyarimana declared that, for the first time in her history, Burundi had been liberated, and that she was a new country. He meant that Hutus had liberated Burundi. Ndadaye was educated in Rwanda and had become a front-line cadre of Hutu ideology.

Habyarimana's unsuccessful attempts to stop the implementation of the peace agreement became another cause for extermination of Batutsi in the country. Killings were reported in all the prefectures. An alliance of parties was formed with Hutu-power and CDR at the forefront. Habyarimana, once more, assured political parties that the agreement was a mere paper-draft that could not bar the ideology.

NDADAYE'S DEATH – THE RWANDA RELATIONSHIP:

Many foreign and regional analysts of the socio-political developments in the region have been talking about the inequality that existed in both the pre-colonial and colonial epoch, as the cause of the hatred between the so-called Hutu majority and Tutsi minority. This book completely dismisses this view as utterly lacking in the politico-economic context. I repeat that a natural economy, in any part of the world, has never developed social inequalities. I emphasise that the Batutsi-Bahutu issue in the pre-colonial epoch was an issue of livelihood, known as castes of survival. The colonial question was also analysed. The region had been linked to the colonial economy and yet no classes could emerge from colonialism. Chiefs and kings were mere selfs, supervising the colonial fiefs. The inequality was talked about, therefore, as neither an economic nor a political justification. It is fitting to repeat that the contradiction of Batutsi and Bahutu has been a colonial strategy of turning the people into races, in order to rule them. The Hutu ideology was a belief taught by colonialists to the cultivators of the region, that they had been exploited and tyrannically oppressed by cattle-keepers. The ideology was left to the colonial hangers-on. All the so-called Hutu leaders are a product of that belief and Ndadaye was one of them.

President Buyoya of Burundi organised what he called a democratic election on the order of France. France had replaced Belgium in influencing decisions in Burundi, as well. Soldiers had been training the Burundi army since independence on 1st July 1962. On 1st June 1993, Melchior Ndadaye was elected with his Frodebu party. Sources informed me that the death of Ndadaye was a result of an agreement between the French, Habyarimana and himself, at their secret meeting in the Seychelles. It is said that the Buyoya government had full information of that agreement. Documents that Ndadaye had when he returned from the Seychelles, contained a plan to create a crisis in both Rwanda and Burundi, through the killing of Batutsi, at the same moment, in the two countries, in order to attract world attention to the question of the Hutu-Tutsi element and the politics of the region. It was also a plan to prevent the RPF in Rwanda from taking power, after the French and their Kigali agents had been defeated by the front on the battle field, and in Arusha, the revelation could not be supported by documentations, since getting them was near impossible. But the saying that the past teaches the present can be a reference to the revelation.

The first extermination of the Batutsi in Rwanda made the Batutsi conscious of the Hutu ideology, and that is why the Nyangoma plan in the 1960s and the Kayibanda-Ndadaye plan of the Republic of the Sun, did not succeed in Burundi. The death of Ndadaye on 21st October 1993 and the death of President Ntaryamira on April 6th 1994, who had replaced Ndadaye, clearly revealed the plan of the Hutu ideological concept. It has to be remembered that immediately after the election of Ndadaye, the French told Habyarimana to send Captain Paul Barril to advise Ndadaye. Barril, as we shall learn later, was an advisor to Habyarimana and his wife. One can therefore deduce that Ndadaye was at the forefront struggle for the implementation of principles of the Hutu ideology. After his death, Hutu leaders organised the killings of Tutsi in the countryside and 150,000 deaths were reported. Hutu civilians, urban workers and students fled to Rwanda, thinking that the Tutsi would take revenge.

In Rwanda, the political-crisis in Burundi became an objective upon which they based the rejection of the Arusha accord. On the 23rd October 1993, Frodward Karamira, the MDR vice president, called for a meeting to support what he called, "the people of Burundi". He called for Hutu unity and solidarity against the enemy Tutsi. Interviewed by journalists about the Burundi crisis, the prime minister, Agathe Uwiringiyimana, gave a statement similar to that of Frodward Karamira. She said that the government was trying to prevent the people from taking revenge. CDR declared that the time for a clean-up had come. Agathe has been made a national hero to the surprise of many!

Radio RTLM, set up by the regime to propagate the Hutu doctrine, called for a decisive action or extermination of all the Tutsi! The RPF issued communiqués condemning the killing of Ndadaye and another strongly warning the regime for a massacre of innocent people in the country. Tutsi massacres were reported in November 1993, in the prefectures of Butare and Kigali. Demonstrations were organised by CDR, MRND and MDR power in all the towns. The government of Mrs Agathe Uwilingiyimana defended itself by saying that extremists carried out the massacres and demonstrations. I have time and again dismissed the extremism concept. I think actions are a direct reflection of a belief condition. There is nothing like a natural state of mind. The RPF also warned Habyarimana and his masters for training and arming the population, and for purchasing weapons continuously, thus, breaking the Arusha agreement.

In Kigali, UNAMIR, or UN Assistance Mission to Rwanda, started arriving in November 1993, with a Cameroonian Jacques-Roger Booh-Booh, as head of the mission. Booh-Booh wanted to include CDR in the government to be formed, against the Arusha agreement. The RPF angrily rejected the proposal and called Booh-Booh an agent of the French. The Belgian minister for international cooperation arrived in Kigali, to see Habyarimana, and to express his country's concern about the arming of civilians and the refusal to implement the Arusha agreement.

THE RPF'S NEW LEADERSHIP

In Byumba, where RPF had an operational base, opposition parties were invited to attend the inauguration of the new leaders of the front, the appointment of RPF ministers and members of the new parliament. The inauguration was attended by MDR, PL, PSD and PDI delegations. The leaders of the front were as follows:

- Colonel Alex Kanyarengwe: the chairman
- Patrick Mazimpaka: the second vice chairman
- Major General Paul Kagame: the RPF commander and RPF first vice chairman
- Denis Polis: the third vice chairman
- Major Theojene Rudasingwa: the secretary general
- Anthony Mugesera: secretary for planning
- Musoni Protais: secretary for mobilisation
- Captain Tega: secretary for youth
- Dr Rwamasirabo: secretary for health
- Anne Gahongayire: secretary for women
- Alloysia Inyumba: secretary for finance

The Ministers of RPF were also appointed:

- Alex Kanyarengwe
- Pasteur Bizimungu
- Seth Sendashonga
- Patrick Mazimpaka
- Jacquens Bihozagara
- Major Joseph Karemera

- Aloysia Inyumba
- Kayumba Immaculee

The front appointed its members of the coalition parliament, and Major General Paul Kagame gave military ranks to RPF commanders. 600 troops were chosen to go to Kigali for the security of the RPF members of parliament and its ministers in the broad-bases government. The inauguration of the blood-based transitional government was scheduled for 22nd February but on the 21st February 1994, demonstrations in Kigali and killings stopped the occasion. Gatabazi, the P.S.D secretary, was gunned down in the town on the very day. The RPF battalion had arrived in Kigali in November 1993. On 17th February 1994, the UN security council warned Rwanda that its assistance might be stopped if the accord from Arusha was not adhered to. The death of Felicien Gatabazi was followed by fighting between PSD and CDR. Martin Bucyana, the CDR leader, was killed in Butare together with his driver. The implementation of the Arusha agreement was also hampered by Habyarimana's refusal to implement it because CDR was not included in the government. The Belgian defence minister flew to Rwanda and warned Habyarimana that Belgium could not wait any longer for the setting up of the government institution.

On the 28th March, all the ambassadors who were in Arusha when the accord was reached, and the Tanzania facilitator, went to see Habyarimana to express their concern about his refusal to honour the agreement he had signed. Even Russia promised support to the implementation, if Habyarimana accepted the agreement. On the 3rd April 1994, the EU expressed its deep concern about the climate of insecurity in the country, and about the failure of the Habyarimana government to honour the accord. On 4th April 1994, the UN secretary general threatened to re-examine the presence of UN troops in Rwanda, if Habyarimana failed to abide by the Arusha agreement. Habyarimana had to see his brother (Marshal Mobutu Sese Seko of Zaire) for brotherly advice. He flew to Gbadolite together with

Ntaryamira Cyprien of Burundi, for discussions about the warning of RPF, that failure to implement the Arusha agreement would mean the resumption of the armed conflict. Obviously, Habyarimana could not accept to share power with RPF. He was simply formulating strategies to kill all Batutsi in both Burundi and Rwanda, thinking that it would change the contract. He wanted to regionalise the conflict and create a reason to justify the full intervention of the French. He had projected the conflict as a question of the Tutsi minority invading Rwanda. RPF was said to be an organisation of few feudalist Batutsi, who had no justifiable cause to fight for. Plans had been made to exterminate the Tutsi should the RPF attack prove invincible. The plan was to include Burundi with the help of France.

HABYARIMANA'S DEATH AND GENOCIDE

By the time of compiling this historical overview, there were still no certainties about the death of Habyarimana. On 6th April 1994, President Ali Hassan Mwinyi of Tanzania, who was mediating negotiations between Habyarimana's government and the patriotic front, called for a meeting to discuss about the implementation of a peace agreement and the situation in Burundi. The meeting was attended by:

- President Yoweri Museveni of Uganda
- President Hassan Mwinyi of Tanzania
- President Juvenal Habyarimana of Rwanda
- President Cyprien Ntaryamira of Burundi
- Vice President George Saitoti of Kenya

The meeting was supposed to discuss the Burundi crisis, but it turned out to be an attack on Habyarimana for refusing to abide by the agreement. President Museveni threatened Habyarimana that action would be taken if he continued to sabotage the agreement. Presidents

Habyarimana and Ntaryamira left immediately for Kigali. They were seen off at the Dar es Salaam airport by Museveni. It was said that Habyarimana had arranged with Ntaryamira in Gbadolite, when they met Mobutu, to kill Batutsi on the same day. Ntaryamira's family was already in Kigali, in Habyarimana's house. They were going to Gabiro military camp, where Hutus from Burundi were undergoing military training. They were to be used to start the killings in Burundi and were to be assisted by Rwanda and Zaire troops.

The plan in Rwanda had been made, and it was even known by the UNAMIR and foreign missions that were operating in Rwanda. At about 8.30pm local time, when the Falcon 50, a French gift to Habyarimana, flown by a three-man French-crew, was coming in low to Kigali airport from Gabiro, it was hit by three missiles from the airport perimeter, crashed in Habyarimana's garden and then burst into flames. All aboard the plane were killed. The time for concluding the social revolution had come.

There are several conflicting speculations about Habyarimana's death. A Belgian journalist by the name of Colette Braeckman, wrote that the plane was shot down by two French soldiers of detachment for training and assistance to Rwanda called Dami. She gave no sources of information, but said that her information was like that of the Belgian prime minister, but denied that findings had implicated the French soldiers. Another speculation was aired by the Rwandan ambassador to Zaire, Mr Sengegera Etienne, supported by members of power group; that the plane was shot by the RPF's Belgian agents in the UNAMIR. Sengegera said that even the Belgian soldiers, who had fired the missiles, had been arrested and killed immediately by the FAR or Rwandan army. He had no evidence at all to support his claim. He said that Belgian soldiers were found in the RPF ranks. Eyewitnesses claimed that white men were seen driving off on Masaka hill, minutes after the plane crash. This claim was not justifiable, because the identity of the white men was not known.

On the 12th of April 1994, the Uganda Democratic Coalition issued a statement from the USA that the plane carrying Habyarimana and his top aids, was shot down by the RPF. The coalition was said to be an anti-Museveni group from the north of Uganda. The group accused the Clinton administration of supporting Museveni. The coalition said that some top aids to President Clinton had conspired with Museveni and RPF leaders to kill Habyarimana. In a statement to the foreign mission and to the American press, the USA were accused of training the RPF guerrillas to destabilise African countries and convincing Museveni to kill Habyarimana. Another statement was made by a French advisor to Mme Agathe Habyarimana, Captain Paul Barril, on 28th June 1994. He claimed that the plane carrying Habyarimana and his top aids, was shot down by RPF terrorists. He claimed to get the information from a black box made by a British campaign, Litton. He asserted that the voices recorded were of the RPF. He claimed to be in possession of satellite photographs, showing lorries rushing from Uganda to Rwanda, with arms and troops, on the evening of the assassination of Habyarimana. He also said that the missiles fired from the Masaka hill were RPF's missiles and that the area was under the RPF's control. He claimed he had retrieved the lancers used to shoot the plane down. Finally, Captain Barrin insisted that he knew of tapes in FAR's possession that had RPF's conversations between the unities, which contained voices of Europeans speaking English, but with a Belgian accent. Another claim was that his close associates killed Habyarimana because he had compromised the Hutu cause and betrayed the revolution of 1959, by submitting to the RPF's demands! It said that the death of Habyarimana had been in the news since 1993. Even before, it was said that a foreteller by the name of Magayane had told Habyarimana that he was to be killed in March 1993, and Magayane was killed on the order of Habyarimana!

In February 1994, a newspaper by the name of *Kangura* wrote about a plot to assassinate him. The claim had it that Habyarimana was killed as a plan to exterminate all Batutsi, because the plan existed and even the UNAMIR and the so-called international community knew of the plan! Jean Birara, who was the central bank governor, had told the Belgian ambassador about the plan. It was revealed to him by his close relative, Colonel Deogratias Nsabimana, the then FAR commandant.

Who killed Habyarimana then, and why? What about the views about his death? All the above and many other claims have proved to be mere speculations. Even those people who have claimed to be members of the Rwanda Patriotic Front, have totally failed to justify their repeated claim that the plane was shot down by the RPF! The Belgian journalist claim, that the plane was shot down by two French soldiers of the Dami, had no political content. Habyarimana had not only been an agent of France, but a trustworthy boy of the West. Even after his death, France continued to support the FAR and CDR, until they were completely defeated by the RPF. There were no reasons why Habyarimana could be killed by his masters!

Habyarimana had been what his predecessor Kayibanda had been, as far as the Hutu ideology was concerned. That is why I think, as a political analyst, that the possibility of Habyarimana being killed by his fellow compradors could be advanced, since agents of imperialism are very often in sharp conflict, fighting for scraps on the tables of their masters.

What about the claim that Habyarimana died in an area controlled by the RPF? RPF members who deserted the front could not support their statement with evidence. Captain Barril had been an advisor to Agathe Habyarimana and her team. He was sent to Burundi by Habyarimana to advise Ndadaye on the Hutu ideology implementation. After Ndadaye's arrest, Barril escaped back to Rwanda, where he was entrusted with the responsibility of assisting Minani and his FRODEBU members, who fled to Rwanda, to propagate "the Hutu ideology". Captain Barril's speech on French television was later denied by the company that made the plane. He had therefore, every reason to fabricate such evidence as he had to please his masters. He also could have made the statement out of anger because he had lost an important job, and his mission was being questioned by those who had sent him. I would like to think that a liberation front, such as the RPF, fights to overthrow the existing social and economic relation, in order to establish new progressive relations. Killing a leader is not a revolutionary practice, ideologically. To say that his collaborators killed Habyarimana, is not an acceptable speculation because, it is said that they decided to assassinate him because he had sold Rwanda to the Tutsi! It has to be remembered that Habyarimana was not only an intermediary hanger-on of the French, Belgians and others, but he had been their mercenary at the forefront. Nobody, therefore, could be more obedient or a better disciple than Habyarimana. He was a co-retainer with Kayibanda, and he even claimed that he crushed feudalism in 1959. He had been asserting that Tutsi were foreigners, who invaded and colonised Rwanda for 400 years. RPF was called an invading force.

Habyarimana assured the Hutu, in Gabiro in 1991, that they were going to gain revenge. He meant that the Tutsi would be killed. In Ruhengeri, he repeated that the youth would defend the country! He was leading to genocide if RPF continued to advance. RPF had overrun the Ruhengeri military camp. He called the pre-arrangement, signed in Arusha a mere piece of paper work. These and other statements are clear indicators that Habyarimana was a leading implementer of the Hutu ideology. His fellow agents could not kill him because they knew that he was their representative to the masters, and to an active cadre.

The death of Habyarimana, therefore, has been a justifiable subject of speculation, and many believe that it will remain so for a long time to come!

AFRICA: SOME TRUTH AND JUSTICE FOR RWANDA AT LAST

ANALYSIS

Who shot down President Habyarimana's plane, triggering the 1994 genocide? A report by two French judges had definitively resolved one of the controversial mysteries of the late twentieth century. Above all, the historical record is now finally clear and beyond dispute. Hutu extremists like Leo Mugesera were deliberately contrived to stir up lethal anti-Tutsi hysteria. Their plot to exterminate all Tutsi gathered increasing support from government and military officials. When president Habyarimana decided he had no choice but to implement the power-sharing arrangement with the RPF as agreed in the Arusha records, the time to strike had come. The extremists shot the president's plane down, and the genocide began.

The Uganda Democratic Coalition claimed that the USA had trained RPF to destabilise Rwanda, Burundi, Uganda, Congo, Angola, Ghana, Kenya and other African states. This is an empty claim. It is an ideological contradiction to call Museveni a Marcist; and at the same time an agent of the USA. Who are those RPF guerrillas trained by the Americans? Paul Kagame went to the USA when he was already a major. A claim of a plan to destabilise Africa was totally myopic because RPF had objective reasons to wage a struggle against a regime that had brought about the struggle as we know it. History advocates the cause of the RPF and knows very well that the Patriotic Army Front was a composition of the real daughters and sons of Rwanda.

THE SECOND GENOCIDE IN RWANDA

Many writers claim that the Rwandan genocide was both political and ethnical. The 1994 genocide organisers themselves insisted that they had to conclude the 1959 social revolution. The Belgians, and later the French, who were determined to exterminate the Tutsi, as earlier indicated in this book, were to conclude the plan, not because of political bias, but more as an ideological mechanism: the coloniser. Ethnic differences were a mere disguise, intended to hoodwink the uninformed into believing that the Hutu were exterminating Tutsi because of their historical differences! The selective nature to annihilate Tutsi in Rwanda has been termed political, and comparable to the annihilation of Red Indians in America, and that of the Jews by Hitler. Questions such as the following expel the comparison between the genocide of Rwanda and those genocides of Indians, Jews, Armenians and the imagined genocide in Cambodia. Were the Jews exterminated by the Nazis because of the struggle waged by the Jews for self-determination? Were the Red Indians in America waging a war to resist the occupation of their lands? Was it an ideological resistance? Were killings in Cambodia a form of genocide or it was mere struggle for liberation against negative forces?

Many books and articles in newspapers have sufficiently analysed and commented on the form of genocide in Rwanda. The definition of genocide in books and in seminars are there for people who desire to read. But it is the author's view that real genocide of the Jews or the Red Indians cannot be compared with the ideological genocide, as a result of the struggle for national self-determination. This book has already indicated that in Rwanda, Belgium had control over the country, and there was no way it could lose it, no matter what resolutions had been taken. Colonialism could only be smashed by an armed revolution, or else it killed whatever it could get hold of. This was the essence of genocide, in Rwanda. Rwanda's shift from classical colonialism to neo-colonialism was a normal process. Local leaders became hangers-on, and ruled the country on strict instructions from the masters in Belgium and France. The retainers did not hide their master's instructions; should the RPF prove to be invincible; a conclusion of the 1959 social revolution would be put into effect!

In 1959, Rwanda National Union had made a cooperation agreement with progressive states and parties elsewhere. Liberation movements were training UNAR's cadres. Internally UNAR had an incomparable support from the entire population. After failing to channel UNAR leadership to comprador use, the Belgians were later forced with an engulfing crisis. This was the basic cause of genocide. Turning the Hutu against the Tutsi was the last resort. The plan had been formulated since the emergence of colonialism. The 1994 genocide was a conclusion of the first genocide that had been badly implemented, as revealed by genocide planners. Genocide in Rwanda, therefore, was not at all political and ethnical, it was more than what many analysts want us to believe.

In a political overview of Rwanda, I have not thought of it as prime importance to list how to organise genocide or to go into the form of the annihilation, but I have found it sufficient to have a glance at what caused genocide. A list of people who organised genocide does not mention the 1959 to 1967 extermination of the Tutsi. African rights gave us a long list of planners of genocide. On 15th May 1994, Robert Kajuga, head of the killing groups, said that the population got angry after the death of their president. This statement is criminally bankrupt and responsible. In the first genocide of 1959-1967, Habyarimana was among the organisers. He confirmed it when he said that he, together with his associates, were lacking in vision to continue crushing the kingdom in 1960! It is thus, vision lacking, to continue saying that feudalism was crushed during colonial rule and that the 1959 genocide was a revolution against feudal rule of the Tutsi! Such statements put some clarity on the politics of genocide in Rwanda. Writers have termed the situation as very complex. The magnitude of the killings, the inhuman brutality applied, the method used to slaughter the Tutsi, the estimated number within a short time, and the politics behind genocide, all made people believe that the Rwandan situation was very complex! What I would like to show in this book is that it was a normal situation; a situation created, first by colonial Belgium and its Catholic Church, and later continued and concluded by the intermediaries that had retained their fief. Several analysts have also been wondering how over one million people could be slaughtered, in the presence of UNAMIR. What about the so-called international community intervention? Where was the RPF? In 1994, the UNO was headed by Boutros Ghali as its secretary general. However, Boutros Ghali had an indirect cooperation with France over the Rwanda crisis. General Romeo Dallaire, from Canada, who was the commander of the UN troops in Rwanda, claimed that he had no mandate to intervene in Rwanda's internal conflict. On 29th April 1994, African Rights quoted Ghali as having said that, in Rwanda, it was the Hutu who were killing the Tutsi, and the Tutsi killing the Hutu, as if it did not matter! I have been emphasising on the fact that a UNO peace-keeping force cannot solve a problem created by a conflict between two opposites, because its creation aimed at preventing liberation and revolution of any movement to capture power. That is also the mission of international community or the capitalist countries.

In the 1960s, Belgium massacred more than 30,000 Tutsi, in the presence of UNO peace mission. The extermination was termed "a Hutu revolution". No voice was heard against that genocide from any Western country. Only radio *Vatican* was alarmed at the human slaughter at the time and called it, in 1960, "the most systematic human massacre witnessed, since the extermination of the Jews by the Nazis!" Why then should writers, and human rights commentators wonder at the accomplice roles played by both UNO and the so-called international community?

Apart from the planners of genocide, the implementers of the plan were not only the state organs but also the churches and the down-trodden masses of the Hutu caste.

When Dismas Nsengiyaremye was still the prime minister, he warned that one million youths would be mobilised to fight the RPF and to teach a lesson to the Tutsi, inside Rwanda, should the RPF continue its offensive against FAR! Habyarimana warned the Tutsi that his Hutu youths would gain revenge. Agathe Uwiringiyimana claimed that the population wanted to kill the Tutsi because Ndadaye had been killed in Burundi! I shall, therefore, continue to stress on the force involved in the Rwandan genocide, in order to dispel misconceptions that the Bahutu had a historical hatred against their Batutsi "black colonisers", and that the 1994 conclusion of genocide was ignited by Habyarimana's death.

When the plane carrying Habyarimana was shot, his army and youths, know as Interahamwe and Impuzamahanga, started the slaughter in Kigali and in the whole country. The Catholic Church was not only the spiritual police of imperialism, as Professor Ngugi wa Thiongo of Kenya called the church in general, but had actively become the political vanguard of colonialism in Rwanda. Its role was openly made clear to me by its participation in the 1994 genocide. I have already said that the Archbishop of Rwanda, Vincent Nsengiyumva, was facilitating by the churches throughout the country. Tutsi families were lured to take refuge in the churches for collection. The Bishop of Rwankeri, Ruhengeri, appealed to the Catholic Church to help the army get rid of the enemy! It is needless to compile a list of people killed in each and every church, many books have those lists.

How they were killed, the tools and weapons used, have repeatedly been referred to. What is essential remains unspoken: why did the church actively partake in the extermination of the Batutsi! That is why I have shown the background of genocide. In his book *History of a Genocide*, from 1959-1994, Gerard Prunier talks about the outside world's attitude towards Rwanda's horror, in April 1994. He says that Belgium did not react because the FAR had killed her soldiers. But Rwandans wondered what reaction Belgium would have taken against Rwanda's genocide. It culminated into exterminating the people in order to cool down the wind of independence. Beligium started the slaughter and it continued. How could Belgium then react against the implementation of her plan? Prunier stated that the USA avoided being entangled in the Rwanda crisis because of the bitter lesson learnt from her disastrous operation in Somalia. Reliable information however, tells me that the USA could not have reacted against one of its allies as well. France, of course, could not abandon its fief until she was smashed by the antagonistic forces of change. Therefore, no reactions of any type could be expected from the forces that had turned Rwanda into a play ground and what she has been from the time of colonial occupation to the conclusion of genocide in 1994.

THE BAGOSORA'S CARETAKER GOVERNMANT

During the night of the 7th and 8th April 1994, immediately after the death of Habyarimana, Col Bagosora, who was an associate of the genocide planners, together with Colonel Rwagafirita, formed what they termed a committee for Public salvation. The reference was clear as he was mistakenly revealing the plan to exterminate the Batutsi. Analysts say that any attempt to challenge neo-colonial intermidiaries and their masters was a direct invitation of cannibalism. It was cannibal action that Bagosora was disclosing.

On the 9th of April 1994, Bagosora and Rwagafirita's caretaker administration was formed, headed by the speaker of the national assembly, Mr Sindikubwabo with Jean Kambanda as his prime minister. The composition of the so-called government was made of MRND, MDR, PL, PSD and PDS. After the formation of his administration, Bagosora authorised to announce a massive "clear-up". It meant slaughtering all the Batutsi and Bahutu leaders thought to be sympathetic to the RPF's cause. Kambanda, who was nominated as prime minister, went on the radio to order a "clean up". Many prominent Hutu were also killed. They included:

- Agathe Uwilingiyimana, the prime minister
- Frederic Nzamurambaho, the PSD leader
- Ngulinzira Boniface, the foreign minister
- Rucogoza Faustin, minister for information

- Dr Gafaranga of PSD
- Felicien Ngango also a PSD member

In many centres people were massacred. In churches where a large number of Tutsi had taken refuge, soldiers threw bombs on them and even children were not left alive. Listing methods of killing and the number killed in every community or village, town and centre, is not my intention. After all, that is what many writers of the Rwanda genocide have been able to do. What has not been exposed is the real cause of implementation of genocide. I have touched on the fundamental cause of genocide, rather than talking about the Tutsi-Hutu hatred and racial differences. It is said that this genocide was perpetrated in the presence of UNAMIR that had about 2,500 soldiers. They were sent to Rwanda to intervene, not to prevent or stop genocide, but to stop the RPF from taking power. The front had declared war against genocide, but after waiting for the UNO reaction, that was inactive.

THE RPF' S DECLARATION OF WAR

In Kigali, the RPF had a strong force of 600 soldiers, sent as a protective force for the security of its political group, that was to be sent to form a joint government with internal parties. The battalion had been attacked by FAR, since the afternoon of the 7th April 1994, and in the morning of 8th April, the battalion decided to come out of the parliament buildings and fight the FAR. They clashed at the Amahoro stadium and in the barracks of Kimihurura. In the Byumba province, Major General Paul Kagame, the overall commander of the RPF, declared the resumption of the war on the 8th April of the 1994. He gave a strong warning to any foreign intervention. He said that any country trying to come to the rescue of criminal forces would be treated as another genocide itself. After the declaration, the RPA started moving down from the North. On that very day, the French air force planes were depositing French troops directly at Kigali airport and Belgium sent another force immediately. RPA, however, had already launched an offensive to stop genocide single-handedly, and to liberate the country. On 11th of April, the RPF crossed the Nyabarongo River towards Gitarama. The FAR could only try to resist in Kigali.

Instead of mobilising troops to stop genocide, the UNO called for a ceasefire, and an official of the French government, known as Bernard Kouchner, declared that a ceasefire and peace were already in the capital Kigali, after overrunning the province of Ruhengeri, Byumba and Kibungo. By 22nd April 1994, the RPF had reached the Tanzania border in Kibungo province. The FAR had already fled to Gitarama. In many areas of the capital and prefectures, the RPF rescued many people as the FAR were fleeing to the south. Colonel Gatsinzi of the FAR, was sent to negotiate with the RPF, but the negotiation did not reach any agreement. Gatsinzi negotiated the release of prisoners, and Colonel Frank Mugambage, of the RPF, persuaded Gatsinzi to disassociate himself and his battalion from the criminal FAR, and join the RPF! On 30th May 1991, Kabwayi, the head of the church centre, was overrun by the RPF.

The Catholic centre of Kabwayi was known for its initiative in formulating the anti-Tutsi policy, and for making plans to exterminate them from as early as 1924 to 1994! During my discussion with a number of knowledgeable Banyarwanda, both in Rwanda and in the diaspora, I have found that there were many people who knew about our history and some would make good politicians. They said: "We remember very well that in order to convert Africans to Christianity, missionaries had to acquire political, economical, cultural and even social powers, as per their assignment by the colonising powers."

In 1889, Bishop Hirth managed to enter Rwanda and score an unwritten contract with the king for the evangelization of Rwanda. The history of the churches in Africa tell us that colonisation had to use both force and conviction to attain its goals. In Rwanda, therefore, colonial and neo-colonial authorities had to involve the churches in the politics of Rwanda. That is why Bishop Perraudin of Kabwayi was the leading planner of genocide from 1959-1967 in Rwanda. This war and this genocide, which in part created by the Catholic Church, lasted for years and years. Like other Rwandans who lost their lives, Mgr. Vincent Nsengiyumva was killed on 3rd June 1994, together with Bishop Thaddee Nsengiyumva and Joseph Ruzindana.

Habyarimana had a special relationship with Vincent Nsengiyumva. Apart from being a special advisor to Habyarimana, he was a business associate with the brothers-in-law of Habyarimana and an activist of the MRND party, as a member of its supreme organ. He was an anti-Batutsi of the first class, according to people close to the Catholic Church leadership in Rwanda. Some people told me that the "wage" of his criminal record in the politics of genocide, was the "death" he deserved! Even those who were killed with him in the meeting room were his accomplices, according to reliable sources.

In discussion with the RPF leadership of the time, I was educated at the concept of liberation. That no genuine liberation movements aim at killing reactionary leaders! That the movements aim at annihilating the state power, in order to establish new progressive relations. But the probability of individual soldiers taking the revolutionary law into their own hands, and taking revenge because their parents, relatives and families were slaughtered in the churches, would not be ruled out. The front's leadership vowed to investigate and to punish the soldiers, in accordance with the rules and fundamental ethics of the revolution.

On June 13th 1994, the town of Gitarama, where Bagosora's government had taken refuge, was overrun by the victorious RPF. The government fled to Gisenyi and France announced its intervention decision. On 16th June 1994, the RPF's radio *Muhabura* was quick to react against France's decision to send troops to Rwanda. The announcement said that France wanted to send troops to save its criminal regime from collapsing; after assisting the regime to commit genocide. While the Patriotic army had almost stopped genocide, France and its agents in Africa and the so-called international comet, apart from OAU, were planning to stop the front from taking the state power. France had already resolved to come to the rescue of its agents. Presidents Eyadema and Mobutu supported the French intervention. Togo and Zaire had tried to fight the RPF and were defeated on the battlefield. The president of the international committee of the Red Cross, Mr Somaruga Cornelio was alarmed that the international community had disappeared from Rwanda, and that his organisation had never, in history, seen such hatred, resulting in the extermination of a civilian population. This analysis of a hatred of the Hutu to the Tutsi is totally wrong. Why had that hatred waited for Belgians, the French and their church to develop? But a person of Somaruga's status had to blame the victim! There are even some Rwandan elites with the same perception.

Belgium had repatriated its troops who were in the UNAMIR, after ten soldiers were killed by Rwandan forces. They were guarding Madame Agathe, the prime minister. After all, Belgium could not oppose the French intervention. The national question in Rwanda is, first and foremost, a creation of Belgium. France is ranked number two in the development and complication of the national question. Writers from the USA claim they were supporting the Patriotic Front! But why then did they avoid the involvement to save lives? Was it because they had learnt a lesson from Somalia 1993, as others writers have concluded? The answer is no! I already made it clear that the USA was not a RPF mentor, and that instead was another active master of Habyarimana that could not, therefore, react immediately to France's intervention because of its interest in Rwanda.

Since Habyarimana had died, the USA had not yet identified a new agent. She had to wait and see. The UNO under Boutros Ghari, was under the French leadership. It decided to send other troops in Rwanda. The USA opposed the move, and Boutros Ghari said that, after all: "it was a Hutu vs. Tutsi problem. Hutu were killing Tutsi, and Tutsi were killing a Hutu!" A statement by African Rights on 29th April contained this declaration. Ghari invited Jerome Bicamumpaka, a member of the genocide interim government, to address the UN general assembly. Boutros Ghari convinced the general assembly on 6th

June 1994 to pass resolution 918, to send 5,500 troops to Rwanda. Yet in April, he had reduced the UN force to 270 men as the genocide was about to start. Belgium refused to receive Foreign Minister Jerome Bicamumpaka and CDR leader, Jean-Bosco Barayagwiza, not because they were genocidaires, but because their group had alleged that Belgium had killed Habyarimana. They were to be received, if they apologised. France, on the other hand, welcomed and had called these men to Paris. They held lengthy talks with President Mitterrand, Prime Minister Balladur and Foreign Minister Alain Juppe on 27th April 1994. On 23rd May 1994, France made a statement about its intervention. The statement said that there was no way that the Great Lakes region could be left in the hands of Museveni and that is why France had supported Habyarimana, and now that he was no longer, France had to use Mobutu of Zaire to stand up against Museveni, who was supported by the Americans, in his attempt to take over Rwanda!

On June 16th, France declared its decision to intervene in Rwanda. In an article in the French newspaper, *Le Liberation*, the French foreign minister said that: "France had not given up its Rwanda, even after being humiliated by the RPF in the battle field! She had decided to fight with full force once more."

THE OPERATION TURQUOISE

On the 23rd June 1994, the UN security council voted Resolution 929 on the manipulation of France and gave the French an intervention mandate. It was said that the French intervention was prompted by President Nelson Mandela's statement, at the Tunis meeting of the OAU. Mandela, then the President of the Republic of South Africa, referred to the Rwanda genocide as an insult and shame to Africa. He said that an immediate action to stop genocide was necessary. It was said that the French took Mandela's statement as another intention of an English speaking leader, to intervene in the French-speaking Rwanda and that Mandela was considered another Museveni.

It was true that the French were competing with the Americans and the British in the Great Lakes region, but that competition was like mere secondary conflict, rather than being a primary conflict. The French's principal aim was to stop the RPF from taking the country. The French were claiming that they were intervening to save the lives of the remaining Tutsi. The Patriotic Front opposed the involvement, saying that it was an attempt to hijack its victory, over genocide forces. It is said that in the contacts with French officials, the Patriotic Front leadership had differences. Jacques Bihozagara, who was the RPF's chief representative in Europe, was termed very accommodating by the French because they claimed he was speaking French. Bihozagara wanted an assurance that their troops would not fight the RPF. Even Colonel Frank Mugambage, who was taken to be the second officer in commander of the RPA, was not opposed to the French intervention, provided that it was purely humanitarian. But the RPF's secretary general, Dr Rudasingwa, who was hated by the French, calling him an agent of Museveni, bitterly opposed the intervention of the French, terming it an attempt to save the criminals. Dr Rudasingwa's bitterness was based on the past record of France in Rwanda. Even Faustin Twagiramungu, who had been rescued by the RPF, condemned the French intervention from Montreal, Canada, where he had gone to exile. The OAU, basing their decision on Colonel Mugambage's declaration that he was not opposed to the mission of the French troops, resolved to support the French's effort!

In the capital Kigali, General Romeo Dalaire of the UNAMIR was not happy about the French intervention, because it was said he knew their deals with FAR. He knew that the French had trained the Interahamwe, that they had actively fought the RPF, and that they were still delivering arms to their defeated FAR. On the other hand, Amnesty International wrote a statement in the death squads in Rwanda, that France was Habyarimana's advisor and participated in the formation of the squads. Apart from her African lackeys, France had no support to intervene in Rwanda from other members of the security council. President Omar Bongo of Gabon called for an interposition force. Tunisia offered troops for operation. Senegal was at the forefront to send troops. Mauritania promised a medical team for the operation. Mobutu was ready to provide both troops and a base for the operation. Togo's troops were ready to move to Rwanda, should France call for more help. Italy was the only country that had promised support to France, but later witheld her support without any clear reason. France decided to launch their operations from Goma and Bukavu, in Zaire-DRC. A force of 2,500 troops entered Gikongoro prefecture and were welcomed by the chanting of FAR and Interahamwe. They also made a quick incursion in Gisenyi. The French were taken to be saviors, to the extent that a French soldier protested at being cheered along by what he called murders. On the 27th June 1994, the French were in Kibuye. It is said that, when the French soldiers reached Kibuye, they persuaded Batutsi hidden in Bisesero; where they had resisted the genocidaires to come out. They were all handed over to the Interahamwe, and were slaughtered. Other Tutsi came out voluntarily to seek help from the French, but the humanitarian mission of the French was a mere cover-up!

Many have written about the killings in the communes where the French were operating. The question is why they failed to keep their lackeys in power? Many analysts have said that, after saving 8,000 Batutsi, in Kibuye, their humanitarian mission was accomplished. Others have dismissed this view as bearing no political content. Unconfirmed reports were of the view that when the French troops entered Rwanda, Britain sent a battalion to Kigali, and USA troops arrived in Uganda! It is thought that France might have feared such movement of troops. The French decided to withdraw their troops for fear of confrontation with Britain and the USA. Although not justifiable, the view of fearing confrontation could not be dismissed because of its political reality. Ideological analysts say that revolutionaries use contradictions between imperialists to gain political power. France, the USA and Britain were very active in the politics of the Great Lakes region, at the time. The situation exploited by the RPF leadership or a move by Museveni, is of little significance.

What is important is that the French were defeated, and the RPF was able to capture state power. That is how the political strategy of dividing the people of Rwanda, in order to make them tools of France-Belgian ambitions and influence, came to a halt. Books have given us a list of people slaughtered in the French zone.

THE NEW GOVERNMENT IN RWANDA

The remaining FAR was uprooted from the capital, Kigali, on July 4th 1994. Gisenyi fell to the RPF on the 11th and Ruhengeri on the 13th of July. The FAR had forced 1.5 million people, from other prefectures, to move to Gisenyi. They were later forced to cross to Goma in Zaire. In Goma, Augustin Bizimungu, the so-called FAR commander, declared that the FAR would rule over a mere desert. That was the plan of the genocidaires. They wanted to show that the front had no support of the Hutu, after exterminating the Tutsi. The new RPF government of national unity was formed on 19th July 1994 and became RPA. After over a million people were killed, another 1.5 million people had left Zaire, and 1.2 million were in the French occupied territory. Was the unity based on the Hutu and Tutsi a reality? Was it a unity of political parties? Was it a democratic unity of differing interests? I think that the process of struggling for and taking over power had been realised. That it was the task of the front's leadership to set up an administration of national unity based on the concrete historical conditions of the country. That concrete analysis of the reality of the Rwanda society, dictated the methodology used to form a government of national unity.

In analysing, I say that the Hutu-Tutsi question is a socio-economic reality, turned into a political tool by colonialists and their church, to accomplish their mission. The government, therefore, had to contain a Hutu-Tutsi element. It had to accommodate multi-party reality and had to retain its vision of a new democracy. This meant that it must be a new national democratic revolution, as I understand it; new because it was different from the first struggle for national self-determination by the previous forces; national because it was mobilising all the forces that could be united, in order to isolate the principal enemy; democratic because the front was an alliance of forces with differing interests, in order to put an end to national oppression.

However, I learnt that it was the front that had to act as the custodian of the revolution and its continuity. It would have been self-defeating to leave members of other parties out of the government. Revolutionaries are aware that after taking the state power, the decision-makers have to retain the drive of all political events, so that confusion among progressive ranks is avoided. Chou En-Lai of China warned revolutionaries that they should not give a chance to opportunists to warm their way into decision-making ranks. It is necessary that the leadership in such governments of national unity have to remain in the hands of progressives, who have to organise the people's power and set up the administration. This is exactly what happened in Rwanda.

The Patriotic Front was an alliance of many groups: rightists, leftists, groups from the west, from Burundi, Zaire, Tanzania, Kenya and those from inside Rwanda. Those from inside the country included people like Bizimungu Pasteur, who had joined the RPF in Uganda, not because of his revolution vision, but because of his unprincipled conflict with the Habyarimana clique. After all, I learnt that Bizimungu was a relative of Habyarimana and a brother of Colonel Mayuya. Another person who had earlier been an active RPF member was Jean Shyirambere Barahinyura. He was also recruited by the front's leadership because of a book he had written: *Le General-Major Habyarimana: Quinze ans de Tyranie et de Tuerrie au Rwanda*. The book talks about Habyarimana's fifteen years of tyrannical rule in Rwanda. Shyirambere later abandoned the RPF, accusing it of being a Tutsi movement. I guess that those who recruited Barahinyura into the ranks of the front, lacked vision because Barahinyura was a direct agent of the French security service. He later became a founder of CDR, a creation of Habyarimana and his clique, to shield Batutsi as a primary contradiction in the country. Some leaders of the front might have based their recruitment of Barahinyura on his education from the Soviet Union, now Russia. Not all Soviet-educated Africans are revolutionary. In fact, most of them have proved to be rightists of the highest order! In the same line of ideas I think that the USSR did not collapse, but was weakened by a leadership with leftist-adventurism, at both party and government level, that lacked a realistic guide to the construction and advancement of socialism. Another RPF member of the leadership who had close links with Rwanda's internal politics was Seth Sendashonga.

After capturing the capital Kigali, a government of national unity was formed by RPF. Parties whose records proved that they had participated in genocide were left out. Those included CDR, MDR and MRND. Ministries that were given to MRND by the Arusha accord, went to the RPF. A new post of vice president was created and General Kagame took the post, in addition of being the first vice chairman of the front and its army chief. He became the most powerful leader in the national unity set-up. The new government had more Hutu than Tutsi caste. It was a socio-political reality that the front had to base its government set-up on, rather than a political set-up. The RPA's government was as follows:

- President Hutu Mr Bizimungu Pasteur: RPA
- Vice president and minister of defence, General Kagame: RPA – a Tutsi
- The prime minister, Mr Twagiramungu Faustin: MDR – a Hutu
- The minister for foreign affairs, Mr Gasana Anastas of MDR and a Hutu
- The minister for finance: MARC Rugenera of PSD – a Hutu.
- The minister for local government, Mr Seth Sendashonga of RPA – a Hutu
- The minister for higher education, Mr Nsengimana Joseph of PL – a Hutu
- The minister of primary education became Piere Celestin Rwigema of MDR – a Hutu

- The minister for rehabilitation and reconstruction for Jacques Bihozagara RPA – a Tutsi
- The minister for transport and communications, Mrs Kayumba Immaculee: RPA – a Tutsi
- The minister of justice, Alphonse-Marie Nkubito of human rights – a Hutu
- The minister of youth and sports, Mr Mazimpaka Patrick of RPA – a Tutsi
- The minister of womens affairs, Ms Aloysie Inyumba of RPA – a Tutsi
- The minister of tourism and environment, Mr Nayinzira Jean-Nepomicen of PDC – a Hutu
- The minister for internal affairs, Mr Kanyarengwe Alex and also the deputy prime minister, chairman of RPA – a Hutu.

When the government was being formed in Kigali, the refugee camps of Rwandans who had become hostages of the French and their forces were being turned into a new training field of militia, together with FAR remnants. Others started their infiltration into the prefectures, neighbouring Zaire. The French troops in the operational zone were busy sending young people who had not fled to Zaire for training. The camps were already harbouring over 2 million people. Before withdrawing their troops, the French wanted the occupied prefectures to become what they termed "a demilitarised zone". On 22nd July 1994, a French delegation was in Rwanda to see Twagiramungu, the prime minister, and the government accepted their condition, providing that they totally withdrew their troops. But in the same month, a contingent of American troops had arrived in Kigali. Some Rwandans were saying that the French started to train Interahamwe, CDR and the youth in general, after realising that they had lost the war. Many camps were set up in Zaire, and the people were forced to obey their former rulers of the genocidal regime. This book commented on how ordinary citizens were forced to flee to Zaire and Tanzania by the criminals, after committing genocide. I have dismissed the view that the RPF was not a liberation movement, but just an adventurous organisation without any revolutionary goal. One of the civilians I met in the camp said in 1994: "Very clever people forced us to flee... the FAR were opening ways with lorries for us. We followed them as others were pushing us from behind with guns... we had to walk like cattle." This statement is an eye-opener. The statement by one of the civilians in the camps put clarity on the saying that the front was not a revolutionary one since it only liberated mountains. A revolution is about taking state power and changing the relations. Tactics used are dictated by the general conditions prevailing in a country. The essence of a revolution is the comprehension of the situation and the fundamental change required, in order to establish new relations. According to the NHC statistics, the number of refugees in the region when the French troops were in the demilitarised zone, were as follows:

- **Burundu – 270,000**
- **Tanzania – 577,000**
- **Uganda – 10,000**
- **Goma – 850,000**
- **Bukavu – 332,000**
- **Uvira – 62,000**

The above exodus was the work of the organisers of genocide. One of them, Barayagwiza, the CDR leader, boasted that "the Rwanda Patriotic Army had scored a military victory." The camps had become military concentrations and genocidal forces had taken control of all of them. The FAR commanders were sent to camps in Tanzania to prepare their supporters to get ready for the invasion. A UN report confirmed the plan. It said that former soldiers of Habyarimana and their militia had control of the camps and had stopped the return of refugees to Rwanda, by force. The report added that an invasion was being organised. The organisers of the invasion had not at all, hidden their plan. On the 7th of October 1994, Augustin Bizimungu, a FAR commander and Mathieu Ngirumpatse, who was the MRND secretary general, threatened to attack Rwanda, should the new government fail to negotiate with them. Colonel Bagosora, who was the de facto ruler or leader of the genocidal forces, was quoted by the *Guardian* as having asserted that he would provoke international disturbances in Rwanda, to coordinate with his previous attacks, in the same way as the Palestian Antifata.

The French government was very happy about the new development in Rwanda. Its satisfaction was expressed by the president's advisor on African affairs, Mr Bruno Dlaye, who told a journalist that the new authorities in Rwanda would not be invited to the Franco-African summit because they were too controversial and that the regime was going to collapse any minute! It has to be remembered that Mobutu had made arrangements in his Gbadolite palace, to take retaliatory action against the new Rwandan government. The following people had met Mobutu, in April 1994 and had advised him of what to do: Mr Herman Cohen, former USA under secretary for Africa, under President George Bush Senior. Herman Cohen had a French wife and was a francophone himself. He was to do the lobbying for Mobutu. Mr Michel Aurillac, a former minister and an African expert for the Chirac regime. Mr Robert Bourgi, a Chirac man and an adviser to Chirac's part on African affairs and on the Middle-East. Mr Jacques Foccart, who had played a role of reconciling Mobutu and his prime minister, Mr Kengo was Dondo in August 1994, when they had disagreed on the Rwanda question. Mr Max-Oliver Cahen, whose father had installed Mobutu to power in the 1960s, and whose role was to advise the Belgians on Africans affairs. The summit was to help Mobutu and his Rwandan friends to score support to attack the new government in Rwanda.

Herman Cohen had to convice the USA government to support the French's position on Rwanda. It was said that Mobutu hated the RPA because the front was a surrogate of President Museveni, and that Museveni was a dangerous revolutionary. The front could create another movement in the Kivu Province because the people in Kivu were Banyarwanda. That Museveni was a well-known supporter of the

Lumumba groups, opposed to Mubutu. Mobutu had been a close friend of Habyarimana, and as such, he had to fight the RPA. The genocidal forces had stolen 17 billion from Rwanda's banks and the money was taken to Mobutu's accounts. But as a political analyst, I have questioned the above reasons given by many writers and observers. One of the political observers said that Mobutu and Habyarimana were among the leading compradors of the continent. They had, together with a number of others, auctioned Africa since independence. Mobutu had an assignment to make sure that the RPA does not rule Rwanda. That the weak organisational capacity of the then Zaire people, had been an instrument of Mobutu and his mentors, that had enabled them to exploit the country and oppress the people (suggest rephrasing).

As mercenary agents, Mobutu and Habyarimana had been seeking armed intervention of their masters, whenever challenged by oppositions. Rwanda is a direct testimony. When forces of patriotism waged a liberation struggle against the Habyarimana's regime in 1990, French, Belgian and Zairean troops came with full force, thinking that they would stop the RPF from capturing the country. When defeated, they resorted to re-training their genocidairies. The Rwanda government continued to fight the infiltrators from Zaire in the prefectures of Gisenyi, Cyangugu, Ruhengeri, Kibuye and even Kigali rural. At the same time, Rwanda warned the ex-army and their supporters that it was becoming necessary to launch attacks at their very bases. A lot has been said about the invasion plans by the French Mobutu and their ex-soldiers in the camps. Infiltrations and fighting have been covered by many writers, particularly in the Kibeho area, in the Iwawa island of Lake Kivu. At Kibeho it was another war itself, suffice to say that, in the camps, a negative force had been created and armed by the French to launch a resistance against the RPA revolution. The Chinese revolution warned all revolutionaries that hangers-on and their masters did not easily give up, after being brushed aside. The revolution's leadership had to know that victory over negative force was impossible without a long struggle. Between forces of positivity and forces of negativity, it could be bloody or bloodless, violent or peaceful. This remains an essential point of my analysis. I mean that the secondary contradiction between the Rwanda people themselves had become the real form of struggle. The essence was the struggle against the real enemy and that is why a war in Zaire broke out.

A PAN-AFRICAN WAR IN ZAIRE

In 1982, one of the leading Pan-African progressives, Professor A.M. Babu of Tanzania, warned African progressives that the national question, in the continent, had a wider perspective than the simple meaning of a nation. Russia's Stalin defined a nation as "a historically constituted, stable community of people, formed on the basis of a common language, territory, economic life, and psychological make-up, manifested in a common culture". Babu said that for historically determined reasons, African nationalism constituted more than Stalin's definition, more than in Asia, India or Iranian nationalism. He said that no European nationalism existed either, but British, French or German nationalism. He said that an African, wherever he/she lived, was categorised by her or his Africanness or his or her colour. The peculiarity was imposed on the Africans by the long and terrible history of slavery and segregation. Professor Babu then advised African leaders that it was due to the African's conscience, his psychology and identity, to know that Africans constituted "a nation", not tics by their territory or common language, but by their physical characteristics. He said that Pan-Africanism was a result of the conditions mentioned above, and that it had a much stronger appeal to all black people, all over the world. He advised that, in Africa, there was no Nagerian, Tanzanian, Ugandan or Rwandan or Congolese Nationalism. He said that a more overriding African nationalism was the only way forward. The most burning questions in Africa today, has been that of waging a Pan-African struggle to liberate countries under the yoke of tyrannical neo-colonial regimes. A Pan-African approach to political problems was suggested by African leaders like Dr Kwame Nkuruma of Ghana, Abdur Nasser of Egypt and Dr Julius Nyerere of Tanzania, in the 1960s. It was only Mwalimu Nyerere who put the principle into practice when he took part in the liberation of Mozambique, Zimbabwe and South Africa. However, after the 1979 war to remove Idi Amini Dada of Uganda from power, Tanzania stood unique in practicing Pan-Africanism. In practical terms, the most peculiar contribution to the principle of overriding nationalism was that of President Museveni of Uganda and his national resistance movement, when he trained and armed the Rwanda Patriotic Front, that liberated Rwanda in 1994. The same contribution was extended to Congo, then Zaire, to remove Mobutu from power. Conditions for Mobutu's removal were prevailing, because he and the French were training and arming the Rwandan forces of genocide. But a Pan-African initiative was to be accompanied by a leadership and vanguard that would have brought about a true subjective condition.

When Mobutu started training genocidaires from Rwanda, at the same time he decided to expel from Zaire, all Kinyarwanda-speaking Zaireans. On 10th August 1996, the governor of Kivu province gave ten days to Zairean Banyarawanda to leave Zaire. After ten days, about 4,000,000 refugees had fled to countries neighbouring Zaire. In Rwanda, the Zaireans formed an alliance or ADFL. On 15th November 1996, the alliance of Democratic Forces for the Liberation of Congo started the war of liberation, supported by the Rwanda Patriotic Army. The Pan-African office in Kampala took an initiative of mobilising progressive African countries against the Mobutu regime. Rwanda acted as the vanguard of liberating Zaire. The RPA invaded camps in Goma and Mugunga and about 600,000 people were repatriated to Rwanda. Some of the remaining Rwandans were taken to another camp towards the North. The camp was also invaded by the RPA and a lot of aminition, arms and confidential files were seized. On the return to Banyarwanda from the camps to Rwanda, President Pasteur Bizimungu said that Bahutu and Batutsi had lived together for 600 years peacefully and that there was no reason why they could not live together then. He had gone to Gisenyi to welcome the returnees. The statement of living together, I thought, was sectarian because, as I have said before, the Hutu vs Tutsi conflict was not based on racial division but a divide and rule policy of colonisers. The castes of livelihood had been turned into races. Bizimungu was another product of the Hutu ideology. Before invading the camps, the genocidaires had slaughtered Batutsi of Congo in Masisi, Moko, Kitchan, and in many other areas. They believed that they were coming back in to Rwanda to do better genocide than before, because most Batutsi in exile were inside Rwanda.

In July 1997, General Kagame, then vice president and minister of defence, warned that if the so-called international community did not stop criminals from killing people and training to attack Rwanda, the Rwandan Patriotic Army had to carry out its obligation. Kagame said that the Rwandan's new help was to pursue, arrest and punish genocidaire. Kagame was given a strong warning by the Francophone countries held in Biaaritz, France, that he was playing with fire by threatening to attack Zaire! In the meeting, President Jacques Chirac of France had asked the delegated for some minutes of silence to remember his Habyarimana. Before mobilising African progressive nations, President Museveni introduced Laurent Kabila to General Kagame. Kabila had been Mobutu's enemy since the 1960s. He had tried, in vain, to fight his regime. He had been living in Tanzania for all those years. In the 1960s, an international revolutionary from Cuba, known as Comrade Che Guevera of Boliva, who had helped Fidel Castro of Cuba to successfully make a revolution, visited the Kabila group in the Congo, with an aim of giving them a comradery assistance, into fight Mobutu. Che found Kabila's group, a total reactionary movement, without ideological theory and application. Che went back to Cuba in disappointment. Museveni, on the other hand, had known Laurent Kabila in Dar-Es-Slaam, Tanzania. He had consulted the Kabila group to buy arms for his Fronasa in the 1970s, to fight Idi Amini. It is said that the Kabila group gave Museveni a lot of arms in the 1970s that were used to attack Idi Amini. Many

Rwandans think, even today, that President Museveni preferred Laurent Kabila, not on merit, but because of his material contribution to Fronasa's struggle! Museveni's critics said that it was self-defeating and leftist-adventurism to propel Kabila to the leadership of a liberation movement, when he knew that Kabila had no vision. Critics say that there was no revolution without revolutionary theory, and that it could not be genuine without principled leadership. A progressive Rwandan says that it was true, that a revolutionary leadership was a pre-requisite for a true revolution. But he reminded the leaders of this volume that Pan-Africanism taught that any revolutionary leader in Africa has an obligation and a progressive duty of taking an initiative, to liberate an African country, when the objective conditions want it.

After destroying camps of the genocidaires in Zaire, the RPA and ADFL continued the persuit of the war towards the North. They were joined, in the campain to get rid of Mobutu, by Pan-African forces from Uganda, Tanzania, Angola, Ethiopia, Zimbabwe, Eritrea, Namibia and Burundi. Reports have added South Africa and Mozambique to the list. Obviously, Mobutu's soldiers could not resist such formidable forces. Mobutu himself was dying of cancer, and the body of his friend Habyarimana was already in Kinshasa, guarded by his soldiers. On learning that the Pan-African forces were near the capital, Mobutu hired an Indian and ordered that Habyarimana's body should be burned. Mobutu fled to Togo and his friend Eyadema helped him to fly to Morocco, where he died of cancer. That was the end of Mobutu and his Zaire.

On 17th May 1997, a new government was set up by the Pan-African forces, through the alliance. Laurent Kabila became the interim leader of the new government. Was Kabila an element of the new horizon of Pan-Africanism? Of course not. He was a mere element of convenience. He could have been faithful to the Pan-African alliance because he had no army of his own. An army is always a leading component of any revolution.

After overthrowing the agent regime of Mobutu, Rwanda, together with her Pan-African allies, were faced with a difficult task of establishing their own machinery of power in the Congo! The alliance had re-named Mobutu's Zaire, the Democratic Republic of Congo. The immediate task could have been the re-organisation of a people's power, followed by the most important task of the country's administration before planning. But Kabila was not equal to the tasks. He had to wait for advice from his mentors. On 17th May 1997, Kabila was appointed by Uganda and Rwanda to head the provisional government, until national elections were held. Rwanda and Uganda had taken the most important initiative to brush Mobutu's regime aside. President Museveni proudly told a journalist in Kinshasa, that the liberation of the Congo was a process of liberating Africa. He was happy that Mobutu became involved in the Rwandan conflict. Mobutu had been the actioning agent of the Congo for thirty-two years. Museveni said that the struggle started by Lumumba in the 1960s, had been concluded. The declaration by Museveni sent a massage to political analysts that, although Laurent Kabila had been entrusted with the affairs of the new Congo, he was not a true and dynamic nationalist. And it did not take long before he turned against his Pan-Africanist creators.

The so-called international community did not recognise the government in Kinshasa. The Europian community, under the influence of France and Belgium, started a complaint that the ADFL and its supporter, the RPA, had slaughtered Rwandan Hutus in Zaire during the war. Commissions were set up by the UNO to investigate the killings. Emma Bonino was a minister of the Europian community. She claimed that the alliance had killed many Hutus in the Congo, then Zaire. The USA sent its ambassador to the UNO, Mr Richardson, to Congo to find out. He went to Kisangani, where Rwandan Hutus were in the camps. He found the camps occupied by women and children. Men had fled to the Central African Republic, Congo-Brazaville and Angola. He had to submit a detailed report in the alleged massacres of the Rwandan Hutus. His report condemned the international community for failing to stop genocide in Rwanda, in 1994. It also accused Mobutu of reorganising the genocidaires, re-training and arming them to invade Rwanda. He recommended a military arrest of criminals and that they should be separated from ordinary Rwandans.

Another team from the UNO were sent on the request of France. Kofi Annan, the UNO's secretary general, directed that their investigations about the killings covered the whole crisis, starting from the time of genocide in Rwanda in 1994. The mission was justifiably refused by the new government in Congo. The mission was an attempt by France to equate genocide committed in 1994, in Rwanda, with the killings of Rwanda Hutus, who had been taken to Congo. After being defeated by the RPA, on the battlefield, France launched a diplomatic offensive saying that Bahutu killed Batutsi, and that Batutsi killed Bahutu, in retaliation, that genocide was two-edged. In Kinshasa, as expected, Laurent Kabila had the task of organising state power. And since this important phase was complex, Kabila failed miserably to apply the dictates of new democracy. He appointed his own relatives and friends, to the most important posts. Nepotism and regionalism became alarmingly noticeable, at the very beginning. His son, Joseph Kabila, now president at the time of writing this book, was made the head of the armed forces.

Kabila managed to divide countries that participated in the Pan-Africanist war, to rid Africa of Mobutu. He accused Rwanda and Uganda of planning to partition the Congo with the aim of creating a Hima-Tutsi empire. He called it a Bantu resistance against the hamitic invasion of the Congo. He went as far as declaring that: "supporting Rwanda's genocide forces was supporting democracy, because Hutu made up the majority in Rwanda". Why then was Kabila able to invite the forces of Pan-Africanism? It is a well-known fact that leftist opportunists always react. Countries like Namibia and Zimbabwe had contributed troops to brush Mobutu's regime aside. Kabila managed to manipulate these two countries, and convinced them to turn against Uganda and Rwanda.

Angola sided with Kabila because Jonas Savimbi had a base in Zaire. Savimbi had been a tool, used by the USA to fight what they thought was a leftist regime in Angola. Savimbi was ideologically formed by the people's Republic of China, but later reacted. Kabila claimed to be a socialist, and had gone to Cuba to look for the support of the Cuban government to fight his enemies. Cuba rejected his request. Socialism, as I can politically assess, is about understanding and changing the world. They say that socialism is based on a working class leadership concept and on economic distribution of wealth.

Che Guevera had classified Kabila among the leading reactionary strugglers in Africa. Put briefly, the Rwandan analysts said that there could be no solution to Mobutu's negative status quo of Kabila. They asserted that Laurent Kabila did not know what leftism was all about: he was an opportunist! Therefore, an attempt to practically apply the principles of Pan-Africanism by Uganda and Rwanda was a wasted effort.

African countries that had brought an end to Mobutu's rule, had embarked on training a new army. Tanzania, Zimbabwe and Uganda started training programs, while Rwanda and Anglola were concerned more with national security. Laurent Kabila managed to convince Zimbabwe's Robert Mugabe and Namibia's Sam Nijoma to support him, in his attempt to send Rwanda and Uganda back home. Their collusion was supported by Angola because of the Savimbi factor. Tanzania refused the collusion because of its alliance with Uganda. Troops from Ethiopia and those from Eretrea had withdrawn, after the completion of their first mission. Laurent Kabila's political bankrupcy made him issue a declaration that he was creating a union of the Bantu people in the region, against Hima Tutsi expansionism.

Rwanda and Uganda were issued with an ultimatum to leave Congo immediately. Since Uganda and Rwanda were the organisers of the Pan-African movement in the Congo, their expulsion was greeted with jubilation by the so-called international community. The ultimatum was followed by the expulsion of all Congolese-speaking Kinyarwanda, from both the army, the ADFL and from the government, including the foreign minister, Dr Bizima Karaha, Moses

Nyarugabo, the vice chairman of ADFL and other government and senior members of the army and ADFL. The agreement was that Rwanda and Uganda had to withdraw after training a new Congolese army and political carders and after organising and conducting national elections. On the other hand, opportunism prevailed over the spirit and strategy of Pan-Africanism. A discussion with Pan-Africanists in Kampala, Uganda, between members of the movement, criticised Uganda for her failure to provide Congo and ADFL with a visionary leadership, since she had taken the subjective initiative of liberating Congo. Other members, however, say that what was mattered at the time, was to brush Mobutu's regime aside so that the country was disconnected from its long-term metropolitan control. The saying that there is no revolution without a revolutionary vanguard, was overridden by the concept of one Africa, and nationalism as a continental rather than a national form.

When armed, ADFL were dismissed by Laurent Kabila from the new army, they started a war of resistance, and Rwanda went to war immediately in support of the rebel's army. It was said that, had Angola not come to rescue Kabila, the rebels could have taken control of the capital, Kinshasa. They withdrew to the East of Congo and started a new offensive against Zimbabwe, Namibia and Angola. Later, Uganda went to war in support of Rwanda and the rebels. A second war of liberation had started. Like Habyarimana of Rwanda, Kabila issued a directive to kill all Batutsi found on the soil of the Democratic Republic of Congo (DRC), as he had renamed Zaire.

Many Rwandan-Congolese were slaughtered in all the provinces, apart from a very small number, who were saved by non-govermental organisations. But it was all in vain. The massacre of people did not stop the rebels from winning one battle after the other. Kabila and his self-styled progressive patrons resorted to peace talks after being humiliatingly defeated by Rwanda and its newly created RCD, the Congolese Rally for Democracy. Sir Kweti Masire, the former President of Botswana, was appointed by both the UNO and OAU, now AU. Lusaka, the capital of Zambia, was chosen as the venue of peace negotiations of the Congo. Kabila was enraged by the choice of Sir Kweti Masire and Lusaka. The rebels, on the other hand, were satisfied by the nomination of Sir Masire, as a mediator. The French and Belgians came in to advise Kabila, to reject the mediation of "an anglophone mediator and a British agent" as they called Sir Kwetu Masire. It was no wonder that Kabila and the new masters rejected Sir Kwetu Masire. Kabila, of course, could not see the real problem of the Congo. He had to refer to the secondary contradiction of Francophone and Anglophone influence. He was unable to get at the heart of the problem; for the problem was that the Congo had increased in power since independence.

The conflict between Pan-Africanists was good news for both the Americans and Europeans. But progressive Rwandans say that the antagonistic conflict between Pan-Africanists, if properly handled, could be transformed into a non-antagonistic conflict, and be solved by peaceful methods. By the time of compiling this book this observation had proved to be factual. South Africa and Mozambique had put all their efforts to find an African solution. Rwanda and Uganda saluted these efforts, because France and Belgium had already approached Mugabe and Nujoma, with the aim of being fully involved in the Congo conflict. They had conviced Kabila to refuse the mediation of Mr Masire. A political Ugandan said that South Africa's involvement in the Congo conflict was President Museveni's initiative, and his attempt to solve the problem by peaceful means. When compiling this short overview, a peace agreement was being held and a provisional government had been put in to place by the South African government. After a few months of fighting, rebels had captured the whole of southern and northern Kivu, some areas of the Katanga in the South, some areas of Kasai and almost the whole of the North. Zimbabwe's arms and soldiers were captured. After being humiliated by Rwanda on the battlefield, Zimbabwe started asking for peace talks.

THE RWANDA VS UGANDA CLASH IN THE CONGO

The second war of liberation in the Congo caused more terrible conflict between Rwanda and Uganda. I have been trying to discover the fundamental cause of the conflict, but many writers and political analysts have differing reasons. Some progressive analysts asserted that the true understanding of the tactics and strategies was the problem, because the situation in the Congo was viewed differently by the two leaderships. They argued that different basic principles were established upon which to wage the joint struggle. This view appeared more convincing than other reasons given by different people in the two countries. A discussion I had with some friends contained many reasons why Rwanda and Uganda fought in the Congo. Some of the views included Rwanda's leadership in the application of Pan-Africanism. Laurent Kabila was a Ugandan product, but became a terrible reactionary, comparable to Habyarimana and Mobutu. Rwanda, as a result, wanted a leadership with at least a minimum concept of a revolution, while Uganda wanted, once more, to impose another Kabila in the name of Professor Wamba, on Rwanda. Rwanda refused to compromise. It is said that this became the real cause of the conflict, for a new leader, for Uganda, insisted that Professor Wamba Dia Wamba had to lead the new movement. Another reason was that Rwanda wrongly assumed that it was the most powerful force in the Congo, and that it was historically linked to the Congo more than Uganda, and that it had to play a leading role in the second liberation. A Ugandan political analyst said that President Museveni was alone in Africa, in terms of ideological perception and that it was, therefore, quite impossible for Rwanda to speak the same language with Uganda, in terms of applying the principles of Pan-Africanism, because of Rwanda's limited vision. The same analyst compared the clash between Uganda and Rwanda, to that of Ethiopia with Eritrea.

The Europian community observers declared that the two countries' conflict was a result of failure to share natural resources looted from the Congo. Both Uganda and Rwanda refuted this allegation. The official of the European Parliament also implicated Namibia and Zimbabwe in the looting. President Sam Nujoma of Namibia angrily accused the West of plundering Congo for centuries, and now making noise, because it had been brought to an end by Pan-African forces. He said that if a commission of inquiry was to be set up, countries in the Congo were to set up a counter-inquiry, on what and how much the West had looted from Congo.

The leadership in Rwanda warned the Ugandan leadership that it was not at all acceptable to play a subsidiary role in the Congo or in any other similar situation. Dr Rudasingwa asserted that they would not accept the teacher-student relationships with Uganda. He was replying to a statement made by Amama Mbabazi, Uganda's minister for defence, when he wrote in Ugandan newspapers that Rwanda had never been thankful of the support given to the RPF to liberate Rwanda. The RPA claimed that the UPDF was treating it as a support force under its commander. The UPDF commanders thought that they had to direct all the operations in Kisangani, and in other areas where they were jointly operating.

The accusations and counter-accusations continued until the two armies fought in Kisangani, in August 1999. Tanzania tried to solve the contradiction peacefully, when President Mukapa met Museveni and Kagame in Mwanza, but the mediation failed to solve the conflict. Other African leaders including Meles Zinawi of Ethiopia, Kisano of Mozambique, Mbeki of South Africa and Izaas Afuoki of Eritrea, also took initiative, but the confrontation intensified. On 10th May 2000, a Ugandan newspaper, *The Monitor*, quoted the overall UPDF Commander Major General Kazin James, as saying that, "In August 1999, the RPA had killed hundreds of UPDF soldier..." but that the UPDF had taken precautions and that if the RPA did not stop their aggressive activities, the UPDF was going to crush the RPA's secretary, Miss Hope Kivengeri. She said that Major General Kazin's warning was not a government declaration, but his own. Major General Paul Kagame himself lamented that Rwanda had left no stone unturned, to find a brotherly solution between the two countries.

On 14th May 2000, the President of Tanzania made an attempt to mediate between Rwanda and Uganda. He invited President Museveni and vice president Paul Kagame. A meeting was held in the town of Mwanza. It was agreed that the UPDF had to withdraw from the city of Kisangani to a town known as Bafaswende, about 200 km from Kisangani while the RPF had to go back to the town of Lubutu, which is 240 km from Kisangani. Some battalions from the two armies had to remain in Kisangani, to keep peace, until the UNO sent peacekeeping forces to replace them. It is to be remembered that when Rwanda and Uganda were clashing in the Congo, Laurent Kabila had already died in 1998. Kabila was assassinated by his bodyguards. The cause of his death was not disclosed. Why and by whom? It is speculated that Kabila's betrayal of the principles that brought him to power cost him his life. He had personally predicted his death. He told a news conference in Kinshasa that he may be killed by his enemies. He was alluding to his turning against Rwanda and Uganda. He went as far as declaring that Tanzania was colliding with Uganda to make Congo their appendage. He told journalists that he had been a freedom fighter for more than forty years, and knew that he would be killed because of that. He said that he had been expecting an assassination. President Museveni of Uganda also predicted Laurent Desire Kabila's death. Addressing a conference of journalists jointly with President Benjamin William Mkapa of Tanzania, after the latter's state visit to Uganda, Museveni told journalists, when asked about the way forward in the Congo, that the Congo conflict would end later, because the problem was simple to solve. He said that in his Ankole community, it was a taboo to all paternalists for cows to come back to the kraal, and to find that their cow-dung was still in the kraal. Museveni called Kabila a "cow-dung"! He meant that Kabila was a passing crowd and that things would settle after his death.

WHO KILLED KABILA?

Some say that Kabila's death was caused by diamond deals and it appeared that Kabila, in a desperated bid for cash, had begun to deal through Lebanese gem traders in Kinshasa. Angola had been implicated in Kabila's death by a number of speculators, but no reason was given for the assassination. Angola had supported Kabila because of her solidarity with Zimbabwe.

THE CONGO OF KABILA JUNIOR

After the assassination of Laurent Kabila, one of his sons, Joseph Kabila, who was the head of Congo's provisional government, was chosen by Robert Mugabe of Zimbabwe, to be the head of the Kinshasa so-called government. That government was only controlling a third of the country. RCD, the Goma movement, was controlling the largest part, while Bemba's MNL was occupying the North. It is said that Joseph Kabila's mother was a Rwandan. His brother claimed that Joseph was not Laurent Kabila's son but his stepson. His step-brother claimed that Joseph's real name was Hypolite Kanambe Kabange, a Rwandan, whose mother was not Laurent's legal wife, but his concubine. Joseph went to school in Uganda, and those who knew him very well asserted that he was very fluent in the Luganda language, which was spoken by the Baganda community of Central Uganda. Joseph received basic military training in Uganda and Rwanda, before the war against Mobutu had broken out. Some Congolese, however, refuted this claim, saying that

Joseph's mother was a Congolese from the Katanga province, the home area of Laurent. Whatever the truth, what is important is that no betterment was expected from Joseph after the death of his father. Political observers are claiming, even today, that Joseph was, and still is, the image of his father.

On a brighter note however, the most heartening development was that South Africa had been fully involved in the solution of conflicts between Pan-African countries in the Congo, and in the peace negotiations. South Africa brought back Sir Kikweti Masire from Botswana and conviced President Mugabe that Masire was the right mediator. Talks were transferred from Zambia to South Africa. South Africa had become the most influential country in the region politically, after her liberation, before Angola was the most powerful force. President Museveni had emerged as a key factor in the liberation of Africa, and a combination of these leading forces had necessarily found a solution for the Congo conflict. The death of Laurent Kabila had, thus, seen the development of both negative and positive experiences, disheartening as well as inspiring, but on balance, the latter had outweighed the former.

The revolution in the Congo had been positive because Pan-Africanism was being applied to the Congo's objective. Political analysts said that the leadership in South Africa had added to the Pan-African impetus. An attempt by the Kinshasa group to replace the mediator, Sir Kweti Masire, by a French-speaking one had failed. The reason was clear. By the time of the Congo revolution, no French-speaking African country was active in Pan-Africanism. It was only in the early 1960s that Ahmed Sekou Toure of Guinea and Ben Bella of Algeria, participated in the Pan-African struggle for self-determination. Since then, no French-speaking leaders have been active in the second liberation of the continent. A new vision for Africa, as Professor A M Babu of Tanzania taught us, was about having a new progressive approach to solve Africa's backwards band dependency conditions. It was, therefore, the new South African leaders that took the initiative to convince President Mugabe, Joseph Kabila's mentor, that it was imperative to continue Congo's peace negotiations. South Africa's role brought back negotiations until they were concluded in early 2003.

On the international scene, France was very disappointed because she could not understand how an Anglophone country could mediate peace negotiations from a Francophone country. The French felt that the British had once more hijacked their fief! Pan-Africanists were satisfied, however, that the process of applying the principles of Pan-Africanism was once more set into motion. In the process of negotiations, contradictions surfaced again, this time between the alliances of Joseph Kabila and Jean-Pierre Bemba, on the one hand, and that of Etienne Tshisekedi and RCD Goma, on the other. Uganda and Rwanda were instrumental in the division of the opposition forces into alliances. South Africa had to reverse the alliance's agreements and new negotiations were reorganised by South Africa. The major items of the negotiations were the sharing of leadership in the provisional administration, the integration of the fighting forces and the arrest of forces of genocide from Rwanda. Rwanda's condition for the withdrawal of its troops from the area it had liberated was that an assurance had to be given, that negative forces – as genocidaires in Kabila's army were called – had to be disarmed, and sent back to Rwanda, to face the legal proceedings. Uganda on her part was satisfied that it had crushed the Allied Democratic Forces (ADF) which had been operating in Western Uganda, with a base in the Congo, during Mobutu and Kabila's rule. Uganda had no conditions in order to withdraw. But a bitter conflict between Rwanda and Uganda, in the Congo, became increasingly difficult to maintain. Genaral Kazini called Rwanda "an enemy" after the clash in August 1999. Rwanda said that her army could not be under the command of the Uganda officers. Bitter exchanges were followed by another clash that saw UPDF losing more than 500 soldiers in the battle in Kisangani. An inquiry set up by the two countries, to investigate the courses of the conflict, headed by Generals Odongo of Uganda and Kayumba of Rwanda, found Uganda guilty of aggression. Uganda rejected the findings, and decided to set another commission up. Thanks to the continued intervention of

President Benjamin Mkapa of Tanzania, the war stopped. But for Uganda, the wind was blowing vengeance and it was almost impossible to sweep it under the carpet!

It became extremely difficult to discover the real causes of antagonism between Rwanda and Uganda. President Museveni termed General Kagame a bankrupt leader. General Kagame said that Museveni's advisors were the cause of the conflict. Writing in the Ugandan newspapers, Amama Mbabazi, Uganda's minister of defence, said that Uganda became a tool used by the RPF leadership to conquer power in Rwanda, and that the RPF leadership had never recognised the contribution of Uganda to liberate Rwanda. He said that the 1960s-1970s Inyenzi movements failed to liberate Rwanda, because they had no extrernal support. Dr Theogene Rudasingwa, the chief of staff at the office of the president at the time, re-acting on Mbabazi's statement, said in a statement in the same newspapers that, "a teacher-student relationship was not acceptable". He wanted a relationship based on equal and principle partnership. Bitter exchanges in the newspapers were later stopped by President Museveni himself. Britain played a mediation role by inviting Museveni and Kagame for discussions. In a BBC interview, Museveni said the labour party of Britain had, for a long time, supported African liberation movements, and that it was not playing a surrogate role to accept the mediation of the Labour party government. Some politicians had criticised Rwanda and Uganda; that they were betraying the African initiative, by seeking a political solution of their separation from Britain. Leftist analysts said that it was very tactical to consult Britain, if a revolution in the Congo had to succeed.

Political analysts saw that the enemity between Rwanda and Uganda was not merely a result of a teacher-student relationship, but that it was caused by the differing views of applying the principles of Pan-Africanism in the Congo. The leadership in Rwanda, according to the analysts, said that the NRM revolution had not succeeded to transform Uganda from the horrifying situation of backwardness, to a long march of building a new democratic Uganda. One of the leaders in Rwanda once said that the problems of Uganda under the NRM leaderships, were that Museveni had become another Kwame Nkruruma in Africa, who articulated the African nationalism, while he had completely failed to marshal forces in his Uganda, to begin steps to change the country. The same Rwandan analysts say that they were finding it hard to understand how a Pan-Africanist revolutionary, of Museveni's calibre and perception, could entrust a revolutionary army to a person like General Kazini. But all the same, the analysts asserted that a revolutionary diplomacy by the Rwandans could save the situation from getting out of hand. The analysts said that the two sides of the Congo conflict were to blame, because people in Rwanda, Uganda and in the Congo wanted revolution. It should have been the guiding principle, and it should have been the main link of the cause.

By the time of compiling this overview of Rwanda, internal and external realities had taken another direction. They had assumed new proportions. Externally, there were no fear of attacks from Rwanda's forces of genocide in Congo any more. Those forces had been stopped by Joseph Kabila because of an agreement to form a national unity government that had been signed in South Africa. A provisional administration had been formed in Kinshasa, with Joseph Kabila heading it, deputised by Azalias Ruberwa, head of the RCD Goma, Jean Pierre Bemba, head of the MLC and two other vice presidents. It had become extremely difficult for Kabila to support Rwanda genocidaires again. Confrotations between Rwanda and Uganda had also ceased. In Burundi, genocidaires had joined FDD and Parpehutu forces, with the aim of capturing power in Burundi and then securing a base to fight the RPA regime in Rwanda. The Burundi strategy of Interahamwe had not been realised. Some members of parliament in Uganda, including Winie Byanyima, wife of Colonel Kiza Besigye, President Museveni's active opponent, claimed that Uganda was training Interahamwe. Uganda refuted the allegation, saying that it could not support criminals. Uganda had also alleged that Kiza's men were in Rwanda under the protection of the RPA government. Later, an agreement to resettle opponents from each country to other countries was reached. Externally, Rwanda's threatening conditions had been neutralised after the agreement to form a unity government in the Congo. Interahamwe and the former army of Habyarimana, which had been fighting for Joseph Kabila, were to be disarmed and sent back to Rwanda to answer charges of crimes against humanity. Joseph Kabila and Robert Mugabe were no longer in control of affairs in Kinshasa. The Rwanda–Uganda crisis had been watered down by President Museveni himself, when he suggested a continued dialogue between the countries, aimed at solving the crisis. In Rwanda, a process of what many thought to be democratisation had been set in motion, by setting up a new commission to draft a constitution. Apart from democratisation after nine years of what was known as an interim period, there was a popular move of transferring power to the people. Some political analysts called the transfer a decentralisation move. Progressive Rwanda praised what they termed the transfer of power to the people through the establishment of people's assemblies or committees, both consulatative and executive organs. Some Rwandans were very happy that the country's leadership had started programs of reconstruction, reconciliation and national unity. They thought that the confrontations were over. Some commissions made up of Rwanda, Uganda and Tanzania delegates were set up to monitor the implementation of the agreement between Uganda and Rwanda.

THE SECOND RPF PHASE

Internally, the leadership was busy, concluding the first phase of national liberation. The phase was concluded by the process of democratisation. Some Rwandans argued that the phase of democratisation was not a new development, but a stage of the second phase of democracy of a new type!

My view was that the formation of a government of national unity was a second phase, the first being the struggle waged by RPA to liberate Rwanda, and democratisation was a third phase of governance which was aimed at integrating Rwanda among world democracies. Progressive

Rwandans, however, dismissed this view. They argued that the first phase of RPF revolution was the establishment of a united front, to a wage an armed struggle against the forces of oppression. They say that the smashing of the oppressive state machine, and the establishment of RPF's own government, was in alliance with others towards a new democracy. They referred to Chairman Mao's proposition that in countries where under development is still the norm; a transitional phase of a new type was the only way foreward. After leading a successful revolution, they asserted the RPF leadership had a long and difficult task of organising the country's state power and establishing the administrative machines. The complex transition period, they continued, had to take into account the external political factors. The contradictions within the socialist camp, especially those in the former soviet union, compelled all leftists the world over, to change their ideological and political applications. African states were forced by capitalist countries, especially the USA, to adopt multipartism: a Western democracy. Political realities in Rwanda, however, could not allow the RPF leadership to immediately introduce multi-party democracy. It took nine years to open the door for political parties, although the Arusha agreement was founded on multi-party governance in the provisional period. Both the interim period of the national unity government and the second period of democratisation were of the same phase. The first phase consitututed a national united front, to smash forces of negativity. The current phase is a second epoch of embarking on developing the country and of creating new relations. This is not a multi-party democracy, but that of a new setting, entailing slow, cautious and systematic steps, to remedy the illness left behind by colonialism and its local ruling agents. Many Rwandans believed that at first RPF's government elections in Rwanda were not new. That they were a step forward to develop new democracy not multi-party development!

Political pluralism within a new democracy is, of course, principles of a revolution. After all, politics is about organising society, about the whole operation of power and about who controls that power. Different interpretations of democracy have been viewed as depending on the rulers' ways of life, their ideas, their principles and their social values.

Even authors of political books have the same interpretations. The most popular interpretations known today are found in the following:

PARLIAMENTARY DEMOCRACY

The advocates of this type of democracy term it a representative system that allows an evolutionary transformation, not revolutionary, to take place. They advocated for reconcillation between capital and labour, in order to achieve industrial peace. It is a reformist democracy of a capitalist nature. Kings and capitalists formed an alliance to rule jointly. In Scandinavian countries, they call it a welfare democracy. It is welfare because capitalists are taxed in order to subsidise social services. It advocates for proportional representations, in which all classes are represented in Parliament. It is a liberal system.

CAPITALIST DEMOCRACY

This type of democracy is a bourgeois multi-party system with various factions, within the same class. Their conflict is not of a socio-economic category, but rather a mere conflict for power. In this democracy, it is only the economic power that achieves political power. The have-nots or the less privileged class, stand no chance of being elected to parliament. The only democratic right the have-nots enjoy, is that of casting votes for the haves, whichever party they come from. It is only the rich who enjoy the benefits of state policies and protection, while the poor are taxed to support government programmes.

ANCIENT DEMOCRACY

Although a kingdom when colonialists invaded it, our pre-colonial Rwanda had not developed a feudal mode of production. Conditions for class formation were non-existent. In Rwanda therefore, fundamental equality without class conflicts was a form of democracy. All communal products were due to collective efforts. On the political scene, kings and their chiefs and heads of clans played the role of elders, rather than that of rulers. Socially, all conditions of life and social matters were arranged through discussions. Although some form of coercion existed, it had no economic content. In essence, it was a paternal form of leadership. The leadership was based on well-known and well-defined customs and traditions. Any deviations from principles of such governance very often led to the removal of a leader, and to the choice of a new one. It was this form of democracy which provided the condition of unity and solidarity when the king saw all his people to be equal as Rwandans, Twa, Tutsi and Hutu.

SOCIALIST DEMOCRACY

Socialist democracy is found in the People's Republic of China, the Democratic Republic of Korea and in other countries with the same ideological conviction. Under socialism, there is a strong belief in the link and inter-dependence between politics and economics. The system advocates for genuine democracy, based on equality of all the means of life. Socialist democracy insists on the power to the people and on equitable distribution of wealth.

NEW DEMOCRACY:

Some Rwandans believe that the new Rwandan leadership had adopted a new type of democracy. UNA's struggle was for self-determination at the political level only. Its struggle was the only form of change possible in those circumstances. UNAR was not struggling to change the society, but to maintain its power in society. It was not a new struggle. Although not new, its struggle was national like that of the new front. All the citizens were mobilised to fight colonial oppression. The only isolated stratum was that of a small clique of genocidaires, who planned and implemented it, and who were agents of Rwanda's external controllers. The RPF is democratic because, apart from bringing all patriotic forces together, it has allowed political parties to operate and compete with it, and after defeating them, it formed a government of national unity. Democracy of a new form, in Rwanda today, has a double task of adopting a general line and linking it with the revolution. The revolution in progressive Rwanda is a new democracy, and the struggle has to continue, through the strategic adoption of a general line, that would lay a foundation for constructing a new Rwanda. Some Rwandans argue that the transitional phase is over and that the front had to rule the country on the orders of a multi-party democracy. But as a nationalist, I think that the new democracy was necessary in an under-developed country, but not in developed countries because to change people's minds to the level of trusting a new system does not happen in a day. More time was needed in order to start another step.

The second phase of transition followed after the liberation of the country and was a difficult task of constructing the revolution. In other words, the second phase must start by talking up the issues affecting the people, politically and economically. The economic task is more difficult than that of winning state power. Already, the administration of the country had been set up by transfering power to the people. Consultative and executive committees, at district and sub-district echelons, are a good reference to people's power. The Senate and National Assembly, in addition to the cabinet, are government organs. They are delegates of the people's assemblies. Rwandan progressives have saluted the transformation of the country. The struggle to solve the people's problems has been accompanied by educating the people through seminars financed by the government. The youth and armed forces have undergone training programs as well in order to raise their political conciousness. Since the economic struggle is a difficult one, it requires slow, systematic and countinous steps, in order to embark on rapid development, without which the country will be plunged into profound economic and political crises. The aim of such rapid formation is to improve, as soon as possible, the well-being of the people, through increased production of material goods. It is necessary, at the new Rwandan phase, that leaders have to create and improve the condition of the people, otherwise it will be a sure way of losing people's confidence. The Belgians and the French had turned Rwanda into their slaughterhouse, as well as their playground. In addition to exterminating a big fraction of its population, it had been manipulated, plundered and exploited, at the expense of the people. Poverty had been taken for granted, with regular interludes of famine and plagues. The enthusiasm exhibited by the people, during the recently included national elections, is an indication that the people of Rwanda may be ignorant, but they are not at all stupid.

Many Rwandans, however, have been questioning the achievement and the revolutionary content of the patriotic front. On the political front, it was alarmed that the Kagame regime had problems including internal contradictions, but their claims are as old as the RPF itself. They refer to the front as a mere grouping of a historical significance only. Some arguments were that there could be no revolution without its theory and a vanguard of professional revolutionaries. It is said that the front had no identifiable vanguard, since its formation. That after seizing state-comprehension, mutual distrust and complete discordance came to the fore, when President Bizimungu and his group formed a political party known as Ubunyanja or PDR (Party for Democracy in Rwanda). Alex Kanyarengwe, the vice chairman of the front, Patrick Mazimpaka and other front-line leaders of the RPF had been humiliatingly sacked. Externally, the sources affirm that Rwanda had no ideological alliance with her immediate neighbours. In a serious discussion with Rwandan progressives, a friend said the Rwandan put clarity on this issue of great concern. He quoted what the Great Lenin of the USSR said in 1990, when confronted with such demands: "And there is no reason to be so much afraid of a struggle. A struggle may cause annoyance to some people, but it will clear the air, define attitudes in a prise and straightforward manner, define which differences are important and which are unimportant, define where people stand..." "... those who are taking a completely different path and those party comrades who differ only on minor points."

Lenin added: "Without struggle, there cannot be a sorting out, and without a sorting out, there cannot be any successful advance nor can there be any lasting unit… an open frank struggle in essential conditions for restoring unity". To wish for struggle without set-backs would be the height of naivety and, if the struggle is waged openly, it will be hundred times better.

The discussion dispelled the question of lack of a vanguard in the RPF, from its inception. Professor M Mamdani had the same view, when he wrote that the RPF liberated mountains instead of liberating the people! An emphasis has been put on the ideological method of worth, of creating a united national front before capturing State-power and a new democracy, after smashing negative forces in power. It is true, however, that a united front must always be under the leadership of accomplished cadres, otherwise it cannot be revolutionary. New democracy, this book has asserted, entails an alliance of many forces to combat the real enemy. This is what the RPF is and was all about. Not everyone in its ranks, such as Pasteur Bizimungu and company, were revolutionary. Some frontline leaderships were an indication that their principles were safeguarded by a visionary group of unprincipeled cadres, at the vanguard. He added that Mandani's failure to understand Rwanda's socio-political was the cause of a mere subjective slogan that makes his book unclear and misleading. The recent formation of a government of national unity, has demonstrated how the leadership in Rwanda is able to apply the principles of a revolutionary strategy. Progressives in Rwanda have found no difficulty in supporting the tactical alliance in order to reconcile the population and construct a new Rwanda.

Externally, the clashes between Rwanda and Uganda have attracted deferring interpretations. Progressive Rwandans say that Rwanda and Uganda were not taking a completely different path, but were not engaged in an open, frank struggle. Another country which is essentially of importance, is Tanzania. This country has been on the frontline in the liberation of most African countries of the South. Tanzania was active in the liberation of Rwanda, mediating the peace talks. It is even now the seat of the International Criminal Tribunal for Rwanda

(ICTR). The relations between Rwanda and Tanzania declined, when Rwanda clashed with Uganda in the Congo. Analysts say that an alliance between Uganda and Tanzania is of a historical nature and that Milton Obote was a close friend of Mwalimu Nyerere in the 1960s, until Obote was ousted by Idi Amini in 1971. Nyerere vowed to return Obote back to power, and he did it in 1980. Tanzania fought Yoweri Museveni's National Resistance Army in Uganda, until Obote was, once more, overthrown by the Okellos, in 1985. When Museveni smashed the military regime, in Kampala, he immediately negotiated a more meaningful political alliance with Tanzania. To date, I am writing that the alliance has taken even more serious measures of a politico-economy union. When the revolution between Rwanda and Uganda got out of hand, Tanzania, of course, had to support Uganda. This was a crisis for Rwanda, because an external support of these two comradely neighbours was of great essence.

Another country neighbouring Rwanda was Congo, up to 2002. (As I am writing this treatise, it is not yet a State yet. It had no role to play in the Great Lakes region as there is no Great Lakes without Congo as it has those great lakes.) The awkward diplomatic situation of Rwanda, as far as regional cooperation was concerned, could not be remembered by her good relations with Kenya. Rwanda had been importing goods and services from Kenya. She had also been training her military officers in Kenya's military schools. Investments from Kenya had been mobilised, but on the political front, Kenya had not much to offer to Rwanda; she had no subsidiary role to play. Kenya was not able to convince Uganda and Tanzania to allow Rwanda to be a member of the East African cooperation. Burundi, on the other hand, was undergoing a Pan-African process of transformation. Like Rwanda, Burundi had been a victim of colonial and neo-colonial manipulations, since her independence from Belgium. Her primary contradiction has been overshadowed by the Hutu vs Tutsi secondary conflict.

The Hutu ideology of Belgian colonial administration was entrusted to Kayibanda, in Rwanda. He made a Hutu alliance with Ngendendumwe and Nyangoma in the 1960s, and later with Colonel

Ndayahoze. Together, they tried to exterminate Tutsi and create a federation known as the "Republic of the Sun". The plan prompted Colonel Michael Michombero to work on the same arrangement, and many Hutu elites in Burundi were killed. Those who took refuge to Rwanda, like Ndadaye, Ntaryamira, Ntibantunganya, Ndayizeye Ntibantunganya, and many others, under went an ideological training in Rwanda, by both Kayibanda and Habyarimana's regimes. Today a movement, known as Parpehutu, is still fighting in Burundi "to liberate the Hutu people"! The new Rwanda, therefore, could not share any affinity, be it ideological or political. The secondary conflict there had attained an even more alarming proportion, but with a hope that African nationalists could change the course of her history. But the question remains, could Burundi embark on a progressive path, while lacking a subjective leadership? My Rwandan friends were focusing on the possibility of creating a regional integration. It is only the concept of Pan-Africanism that can save Burundi. They focused on her membership to the cooperation of East Africa. Similarly, Rwanda is a State and a country, but not a full nation. Her membership to the EAC can liberate her economically, but only if the cooperation is led by a visionary leadership. Rwanda's application to the EAC membership was under consideration. If her confrontation with Uganda was not sorted out, it would be difficult for Rwanda to build and carry forward her revolution, as I assert it. The so-called international community has commended Rwanda's good governance; a form of recognition and good relations with other countries. It is always true that the good governance, which was widely spoken about, was not in form but rather in content.

The second phase of establishing a new democracy did not come prior, but after a successful revolution. The phase was more difficult than the phase of struggle to take over power from negative forces. Chair Man Mao of China, recommended politics first before embarking on the most difficult task of economic construction. The Rwandan leaders, therefore, were on the move, on the journey to transform the country, beginning the complex period by organising the task slowly but surely, systematically and continually. Some

Rwandans were of the view that the RPF had failed in putting politics in command. Their arguments referred to the dismissal of many leaders of the party, such as Alex Kanyarengwe, who was the RPF chairman, Patrick Mazimpaka, the front's vice chairman and de facto leader, Seth Sendashonga, a member of the central committee and many other leading members of the front. They also referred to people of great influence, who were thrown out of the government, such as the former President Pasteur Bizimungu, the former Prime Ministers, Faustin Twagiramungu, Celestin Rwigema, and the speaker of the National Assembly, Sebarenzi-Kabuye, without mentioning ministers, members of parliament and senior officers from the Patriotic army. These critics were alarmed that the second phase to establish new democracy had completely failed. They added that the front's failure is compounded by the hostility between Rwanda and Uganda, and between Congo.

However, what progressive Rwandans say about the failure of the second phase of the RPF's criticisms by some Rwandans, were facile and simplistic. They said that Rwanda had been ruled by a compradorial oppressive machine since independence! They said that the agent class had to be smashed by a national united front. They said that the unity had to be composed of all nationals who could be brought together. They remember that politics was about the study of how to organise people, how to achieve and control power, about who achieves and maintains power, and to which end that power is put. Those who took a subjective initiative to liberate the country were the ones that were acting as vanguard. National realities dictated that Alex Kanyarengwe headed the front, not because he was a revolutionary, but because he was objectively the right person to be put forward as a matter of compromise. However, this compromise brings in negative attitudes of non-initiators, which have to be kept in close check. Chuo-En-Lai, one of the revolutionary leaders of the Chinese revolution, warned all the leaders of genuine revolutions, that their victory over negative forces was impossible without a long, stubborn and desperate "life and death struggle", which meant a bloody and bloodless; violent and peaceful; military and economic;

and educational and cultural struggle.Chuo-En Lai warned revolutionary leaders that they should guard against rightist opportunists, who warn their way into the leadership top echelons, because they were anti-revolution. The teaching of the Chinese revolution was an explanation to why ultra-revolutionary rightists, in the RPF and its government, were thrown out of the leadership. They say that what many people were viewing as the RPF weakness, was quiet organisational. Those who were dismissed and those who were removed from positions of leadership were political pickpockets, whose tricks were discovered and exposed in good time. In agreement with the views expressed by some of my friends, President Kagame told journalists that Bizimungu Pasteur was given "a yellow card first" in the game, but he did not comply, and later, he had to be given a red card that dismissed him from the leadership.

Many leaders, in Rwanda, assert that the second phase of the revolution is over. The phase they affirm is known as, "Inziba Cyuho" or "gap bridging". Those leaders are emphasising that democratic elections marked the end of the interim period, and they gave a democratic mandate to President Kagame and the RPF, to rule the country legally because the interim period had no people's mandate. Political and civil society leaders, therefore agreed that there have been the organisation phase or the formative period when Banyarwanda, in diaspora, organised themselves and developed on ideology of liberation. The second phase, it is affirmed, is that of waging a struggle and smashing the agent regime. Leaders say that the provisional administration formed in 1994 to 2003, marked the third phase of the front. Then, it claimed, comes the fourth phase of democracy after general elections that legalised the front's leadership. As a progressive Rwandan, however, I dismissed the phasing out of the revolution into four periods. I supported the two-phase theory saying that the first phase is characterised by tactical alliance into a united front. Prior to taking state power, any liberation movement must be equipped with revolutionary principles, the vanguard composed of few professional revolutionaries, and there was no revolutionary theory without a revolutionary practice. Therefore the whole process, up to seizing state power, was the first phase of the revolution, known as the united front period, of bringing all the forces together in order to isolate an agent clique. Whether the first phase took more than twenty years, like that of SPLM of John Garang of Sudan, or only four years like that of RPF in Rwanda, the time factor did not determine the essence of the transition. The second phase was correctly written in this book. That phase – new democracy – was a long, historical period full of contradictions and struggles. It was a struggle between the progressive line and a reactionary line: progressive because the RPF had to build a new Rwanda from zero; reactionary because, even those who had participated in the struggle against Habyarimana and company, turned out, as expected in the progressive struggle, to be an ambivalent force.

On the political front, therefore, Rwandan progressives emphasised the reorganisation of the country; the drafting of a people-oriented constitution; the establishment of institutions responsible for accounting and control, and the setting up of machines to educate and unite the people. All these were a means of democratisation of the new revolutionary phase.

I would imagine that the economic task is more difficult than winning the state power. The work is normally slow, systematic and continuously progressive. Nevertheless, the people's well-being must be improved, as soon as possible, through the provision of material goods. Within these last nine years, the RPF has failed to meet this economic target, but has shown that it has a future. As I try to analyse, the condition of the people has not improved much yet, because people are still dying of hunger in some provinces like before. Housing, feeding and clothing the people are the primary needs of a backward society, like the Rwandan society. Without these basics of life, the RPF will lose the confidence and support of the masses, as I have predicted. The front will not retain the people's enthusiasm by merely telling them what it intends to do. They must get commodities and industrial goods. Poverty alleviation means that agriculture has to flourish and must be linked with industrial development. The RPF's programme is about developing an integrated, self-supporting economy. When you speak to anyone in the government they are determined to reach this goal soon or later.

As Rwandan nationalists we are very happy that externally, the leadership is striving to develop conditions for politico-economic integration with communities of the East Africa cooperation. I think that an underdeveloped country like Rwanda can make her revolution triumphant, with only two essential conditions:

- By winning the support and confidence of the masses or people

- By receiving fraternal support from other countries with similar views.

The past years of the new democratic phase, therefore, have seen the development of positive political development, which must be immediately supported by inspiring economic arrangements. Building, not rebuilding, and developing the country step by step, leading to the establishments of small and medium-scale industries, are the surest channels of modernising the country. As the struggle to build and develop a new Rwanda continues relentlessly, Rwandan intellectuals, in the country and abroad, are warning that our culture has been robbed of its values by colonialism which has been at the helm of the society for the last four decades. It is said that the church has been at the forefront in the distortion of our ethics and values. The view is supported by the loss of our ancestral names, and the adoption of names referring to the mercy of God, Jesus and his mother, Mary. Today, names such as the following are an indication of such alienation:

- Twagiramungu, Bizimungu
- Mujawamariya, Nyinawamariya
- Uwamariya, Nzambazamariya
- Uwayezu, Nyinawayezu
- Nduwayezu

Some believe that other names became common only after the invasion of the Catholic Church, such as:

- Habyarimana, Nshimiyimana
- Ndahimana, Kubwimana
- Mbarushimana, Nzabahimana
- Hakizimana, Nsengimana
- Niringiyimana, Ngendahayo
- Ndagijimana, Nahayo, Nyiramana
- Hitimana, Nteziryayo, Niyitegeka
- Twagirumukiza, Ikimpaye

In the 1994 genocide, churches became slaughter chambers because of the alienation. When churches came into Africa we were taught that the House of God is sacred. A prominent church leader, talking about the extermination of Batutsi in churches during the 1994 genocide, said that all the devils had abandoned their fief in Hell and had invaded Rwanda. Would it not be another miracle finding Satan at the altar of the Holy Church? Rwanda had often been referred to as the leading Catholicised country in Africa. Our trust in the Almighty contributed to the rate of death, during genocide. The ministry of youth and culture has not – up to 2002 – set up a programme of transforming our culture, but some intellectuals are advocating going back to our roots of Rwandan culture through Unesco. In discussions with progressive Rwandans you can hear them saying that there was no global or national culture, and that no culture belongs to a particular continent or race. Progressives call culture a totality of a people's attitudes and their psychology; a reflection of a class that ruled a given country. That it was indeed a superstructure of a politico-economic mode.

Before the invasion of Rwanda by colonial powers, the country had a feudal-like system. The culture at the time was a feudal culture, hence the saying that "*Umwambari agenda nka shebuja*" meaning, "a subject walks like his master". Feudal values and aspirations were copied and imitated by the populations. "*Ubuphura*" – or nobility – remains a quality to be imitated by generations. We still adopt names referring to kings and queens and to the kingdom itself, after all these years. Names such as the following still exist:

- Kalibwami, Nzajyibwami
- Karibwami, Mugabowakigeli
- Mukakigeli, Nkundumwami
- Nkuliyingoma, Muvuningoma
- Mukayuhi, Mukamutara
- Nyinawumwami, Mugabekazi
- Mujawingoma, Mukayuhi

In one type of Rwandan culture, at a time in those years of colonial invasion, they adopted names referring to cows such as the following:

- Kiberinka, Ngaruyinka
- Harerinka, Mukobwajana
- Gaju, Niwegaju, Munganyinka
- Kankuyo, Mukasine, Kamusengo

Names of Rwandans are a good reference to the class character of our culture, in addition to all the aspirations and activities of the population. Religion, education, dances and other human activities reflect politico-colonial Rwanda. Rwandans' activities reflect our historical level of advancement: our feudal relations and our means of livelihood. Our songs, poems, dances and other activities were referring to cows or to cattle-keeping, land cultivation and even to hunting. The famous Intore dances today are the passing down of the practices, of the pre-colonial epoch, which were a form of military exercises by the armed forces. Such groups of ballet dancers belonged to the Umwami and the exercises were done on a regular basis. Groups of female ballet dancers belonged to the Queen Mother and used to welcome the army back from the battlefields, after winning a war. Not only were the dances feudal-oriented, but there were poems and recitals as well. They were praising national heroes known as *Intwari,* and royal cows known as *Inyambo.* Education and religion rituals were all based on the royal values and well-being. Culture, therefore, in the pre-colonial epoch, was a feudal culture, cementing feudal relations, and reflecting the means of life. Going back to the roots of our culture, therefore, means re-establishing feudalism and resurrecting all its characteristics. But with time, many of the practices died, while the existing traditions have become stagnant and retrogressive. Such rich dances require a revolutionary orientation.

Rwanda, up to 2003 and even after, was emerging from being a decriminalised agent, to the road of national unity and reconstruction. This general social malaise has entangled the culture in the whole colonial and neo-colonial machination. What many people call modernisation or civilisation; praying, walking and other practices, is culture. It is our culture to date. It is a neo-colonial culture. What intellectuals refer to as Rwandans' culture is a set of mere traditions. The leadership in Rwanda, I insist, must all assess the elements of their rich traditional practices and their true worth. They must be able to transform them into a national culture, based on Rwanda's history and the conquests of the struggle itself. They must decolonise the people through education, cultural practices and cleansing processes. Some Rwandans believe that even Kinyarwanda itself has been distorted by the agent class in power, from Kayibanda-Habyarimana. They say that it is no longer the language that has been developed by Rwandans from the beginning of history, to the time of invasion of the country by colonialism. They suggest that a commission has to be established to correct the blunders made, and to give the country a new national language. It is very true that Kinyarwanda, of the pre-colonial time, is not the Kinyarwanda of the neo-colonial time. The language has undergone a lot of changes to respond to the dictates of the system. But the immediate task, in the new Rwanda, is not to write the language and change names of people, but to develop and raise the political and moral awareness of the people and of patriotism; the spirit of devotion to the cause of the revolution. The task ahead, therefore, is to develop people with a feeling of humanism, solidarity and respect. The new Rwandan leadership has a

167

cultural obligation of distinguishing, within the totality of the people's values, the essential and secondary values, the positive and negative values, and the strong and weak values, in order to make plans, to decolonise the minds of the people, and develop a new culture for a new Rwanda. Otherwise, culture remains a class superstructure of a political system, and hence, a feudal culture, a colonial culture, a neo-colonial culture and a new and progressive culture imposed by a revolution. Those who talk about world culture, racial culture or continental culture, are there to confuse us and disarm us of the consciousness, of how Rwandan culture has been turned into retrogressive or stagnant and decadent tradition. It means, therefore, that there is no possibility of going back to the roots of Rwandans' culture. The elements of old positive values could serve as a starting point for raising a new culture.

CONCLUSION

As said, politics is a study of the organisation of society, the whole operation and machinery of power; how that power is achieved and by whom; which class controls that operation and machinery of power; how that class maintains power and to which end that power is put. This overview of Rwanda is more of her politics than her history. My survey and analysis has mainly been concerned with showing that the organisation of the Rwandan society has never had any Hutu vs Tutsi content, but the whole operation and machinery of power was a natural process; a struggle to harness natural properties to the needs and wants. I have seen that this struggle is the history root of Munyarwanda.

In the pre-colonial epoch, many know that in Rwanda the maintenance of power was not of class, because conditions for class formation, in Rwanda, had not yet developed. The analysis has repeatedly shown that the Hutu-Tutsi phenomenon, as taught by rightist historians, is completely historical and apolitical because castes, created by means of survival, could never be either classes or races. The best means of livelihood happened because of leadership. It was an evolutionary process that took places everywhere. In the Sahara region or in the present Angola, kings emerged from the moors and from the Touaregs, who were cattle-keepers; a development quite similar to that of the Great Lakes region.

Kings in Nagelia emerged from cultivators like Ibo and Yoruba, instead of developing from the Furani community, who were cattle-keepers. The pre-colonial epoch has been that of independent Rwanda under monarchic role, until the system was invaded by colonialists.

The acquisition of colonies, as potential markets and potential outlets for capital, as well as potential sources of raw materials, has been the highlight of the colonial invasion of Rwanda. Beginning in 1884, German colonisers grabbed Rwanda and she became a part of the East African Germany. I dismissed the statement that colonialists were on a civilising mission, terming it misguiding and fallacious. We have seen that, in order to comprehend colonialism, first I have to trace the roots of capitalism itself; a factor that led me to the reasons why monarchic rule had to be completely destroyed, by smashing its materiel base.

My further analysis tried to expose the reason for an antagonistic contradiction between Rwanda rulers and colonialists. It has asserted that in order to rule Rwanda, colonialists had to divide the country using the caste criterion because nutritional differences were an ideal basis for calling Batutsi foreign invaders or black colonialists. The policy of divide and rule was reinforced by brutalisation of the people, deprivation of a sense of self and pride, toiling under inhuman conditions, reducing the resources, disruption of culture and other colonial manouevres which deprived Rwandan nationalists. The Rwandan National Union (UNAR) was the only nationalist movement with an anti-colonialism ideology. To the colonisers, the ideology was a big blow to their colonial aims. It was an engulfing crisis to the Belgian lure. UNAR, having consolidated in the country, started contacts with other anti-colonialism movements in Africa and even with socialist countries of Europe and Asia. I have stressed that the outcome was to turn the people one against the other, while the colonialists made a propaganda that the Hutu were making a revolution against the colonisation by Tutsi. The first genocide from 1959-1962 was a consequence of the threat of losing a territory. Violence is always a last resort.

Since the ground had been prepared, the question to the colonisers was not to allow Rwanda to be independent, but to get local reactionary agents, as colonial hangers-on. We have stressed that Parmehutu was strategically formed by the Catholic Church and the Belgians, to project a picture that the national question was not that of colonial politics, that had fashioned anti-colonial struggle, but was the question of the Tutsi that "had colonised the Hutu, until the Hutu rose up to fight for their rights!" Parmehutu and later MRND were the tools to advance colonisation of a new type, aimed at diverting the idea of self-determination. This book has indicated how the strategy succeeded for three decades, until forces of change smashed it in 1994.

The struggle to start afresh was a development from the first struggle for self-determination. Conditions favouring that struggle were: objective conditions, a political situation and a subjective initiative emphasised, developed from the real needs and interests of the country or her general historical conditions. Internal causes and external conditions existed for struggling, and for attaining or conquering state power. Analysis termed the liberation of Rwanda a two-faced strategy; the struggle against the water in Kigali and a test of the application of the principle of Pan-Africanism. On Friday 12th October 1990, the national newspapers in Kenya, quoted President Museveni, of Uganda from a press conference, on 11th October 1990, that:

> "The Habyarimana Army would not be able to defeat the RPF, which had launched an attack from Uganda: "I doubt very much that the troops, that are there, defeat the rebels... some of them are our best people. In fact the origin of problem is that the government in Rwanda has shut out its borders for two million of its own people."

He said that he had warned Habyarimana, in September 1990, that the large and restive refugee population was a threat to his government: "I told him you should watch out. These boys are very dangerous. They have acquired skills". He told Habyarimana that the boys were likely to desert his army if they saw an opportunity to go home.

In October 1990, in Kenya, an estimate of people killed by the army of Habyarimana, was between 30,000 and 40,000. Rwanda's foreign minister, then Casimir Bizimungu, was also quoted as having told diplomats in Kigali that: "the aim of the rebels RPF was to set up a feudal minority regime". This statement has disclosed the bankruptcy and myopia of the then good boys, in Kigali. The massacre of the Tutsi community at the beginning of the struggle remains a testimony that the second genocide of 1994 was not at all caused by the death of Habyarimana, but by cannibalism continued by the mercenary agents, from the extermination strategy started by Belgium. The genocide of 1959-1962 and that of 1993 were not a result of the death of Habyarimana. As Museveni had warned, the boys became dangerous and the mercenary regime and its army were completely smashed and the RPF emerged victorious.

As expected, the RPF faced both internal and external resistance. The UNO resolution 929, gave France a mandate to invade Rwanda, to stop the Patriotic Front taking power. France trained and armed, once more, and defeated FAR and Interahamwe in Zaire. Forces of resistance started to attack in the provinces of Ruhengeri, Gisenyi, Zairean and Tutsi were killed, the reason being to support France and its defeated FAR. When addressing the Pan-African movement, members in the Rwandan capital of Kigali, the chairman of the movement, Col Kahinda Otafire of Uganda said that Pan-Africanist could not tolerate a regime that expels its own nationals from a country of their ancestors. Revolutionaries claimed that it was impossible to make a revolution without a revolutionary vanguard. In Africa, the Africaans extended nationalism beyond colonially-created borders. President Museveni of Uganda piloted the principles of Pan-Africanism in Zaire, by mobilising countries with a Pan-African vision, to brush the Mobutu dynasty aside. But because leaders of countries that smashed the regime of Mobutu had not the same level of Pan-Africanism, they conflicted for influence in the newly liberated Congo. Kabila was a creature of President Museveni. It is briefly indicated why Kabila had to betray his mentors. He was not visionary. He was tactically installed to the position until a leader with vision was found. Laurent Kabila was killed by his soldiers and was replaced by his son, Joseph Kabila, who analysts believe was chosen by Robert Mugabe of Zimbabwe. The blunder in the application of the principles of nationalism cost Congo dearly. Another conflict, this time between countries, was agreed upon. In the Congo conflict, Joseph had only a third of the Congo. The RCD forces had taken the largest part of the DRC. Eventually, negotiations in South Africa came to a fruitful derision of state and to government posts. Analysts in Rwanda were still insisting that the principle of Pan-Africanism could still be persuaded. But people were doubtful about the Kabila, Ruberwa and Bemba combination. They were wandering whether this alliance could constitute a motive force of the Congolese revolution. The analysis predicts a Pan-African initiative through democratic tactics. The confrontation between Rwanda and Uganda has been a puzzle to nationalists in the two fraternal states and no one has yet been able to explain or discover the cause.

The two phases of the struggle in Rwanda, the analysis asserts, were not a conspiratorial struggle against a democratic regime in Kigali, but a struggle against a negative power over the people. The aim was to establish a power that advanced the interest of people. Chairman Mao of China taught us that the contradiction among the people can, if properly handled, be transformed into a non-antogonistic contradiction. Analysis has given credit to the leadership in Rwanda, for adhering to Mao's teaching. The first phase, the anti-Habyarimana and company's phase, was a united front. It was headed by Alex Kanyarengwe, a former collaborator of Habyarimana, after General Rwigema's assassination. It had people like Pasteur Bizimungu, Colonel Lizinde and Seth Sendashonga, in its top ranks. It also united Rwandans with differing interests. The second phase, new in progress, was of a specific kind. It was a united front under democratic process, of a new type. It was laying the foundations for national construction. The two phases are important for devising tactics and strategies for national reconciliation and development. Analysts felt that the new Rwandan Army, the Rwandan People's Defence Forces (RPDE, formerly RPA,) was courageously bearing the brunt of Africa's principal struggle, especially after brushing the Mobutu and Kabila regimes aside. Thus, the second phase of the RPF's struggle had seen – and is still seeing – the development of both positive and negative experiences, disheartening, as well as inspiring, and on balance, the positive trends have out-weighed the negative ones. These experiences are likely to continue because the negative claims are a product of the past reactionary; while the positive ones are a parcel of the future with progressive programmes of national rebirth, with a Pan-African perspective. The application and endorsement is an example in point. There is no need for Rwanda to be despondent. The leadership has to be continually vigilant and progressively forward-looking, for the struggle has to continue relentlessly.

RWANDA TODAY

After the genocide, a lot of good things have happened to Rwanda as a country in general. Under the leadership of President Kagame, who is a fearless and hard-working man, all areas of life have made a real progress. However, I would like to summarise only five areas: justice, economy, security, education and health of the society.

Many people, especially the outsiders, were worried about the country that was left without anything. No one knew where to start or what to do next. Thank God, who gave our leaders the vision to not be too scared about what happened, but instead they opted to start from scratch. The courage of President Kagame has lead to other countries trying to copy the Rwandan model in many areas such as peace making and economical progress. This can be seen in rural areas where the majority of people are living. They claim to be happier now then before the genocide was committed, even though few people are not yet satisfied because they still don't understand how a Tusti leader will lead them without harming them. This can be seen as a result of brain-washing, based on ethnic hatred, but the majority can't imagine Rwanda without President Kagame.

Even though Rwanda is a poor country like any other many African countries, it was not easy to bring about these two brother enemies. In fact, Rwanda had a problem of people who lost their relatives during the genocide and they were still wounded badly. On the other hand, there were other people who killed their neighbours and yet they were living in the same area. The government was struggling to reconcile those people so that they may live together in order to bring about reconciliation and to promote the economy. The other major problem was that the majority of men were in prison, while waiting for justice. This was because the normal court of justice could take years before taking even a few of the genociders to court. That is why the government decided on using the traditional court called Gacaca. Normally "Gacaca" is a Kinyarwanda word meaning "grasses". Traditionally when there was a problem people did not fight, but they used to call grown-ups or old people in order to sit on these "grasses" and settle the matter between them, regardless of their ethnic background because all of them were seen as Rwandan. The other meaning is that "Gacaca" is the name of a type of grass (*umucaca*) which is strong, especially when you put them together. Previously this court was made up of villagers who the government trusted would achieve the truth and justice. The Gacaca court deals with reconciliation and aims to promote community healing by making the punishment of the killers faster and less expensive to state. According to Jimmy Walter, as stated on Wikepedia, "the mission of this system is to achieve true justice reconciliation. It aims to promote community healing by making the punishment of perpetrators faster and less expensive to state. This is because genocide was done by Rwandans, to other Rwandans, therefore it is them first of all who have to rebuild themselves and the country afterwards in all areas."

According to the official website of the Rwandan government of the national service of Gacaca jurisdictions, the Gacaca court system has the following objective:

1. The reconstruction of what happened during the genocide.

2. The speeding up of the legal proceedings by using as many courts as possible.

BIBLIOGRAPHY

Dalaire Remeo Shake hands with the devil irst publishd in Great Britain in 2004by Arrow books.

Grotremanche Gil A Sunday at the pool in Kigali first published in England in the UK in 2003 by Ganongte book LTD.

Prunia Gerard, The Rwanda crisis, Histoy of a genocide first pulushed in the United Kingdom by C. Hurrst & Co. (Publishers LTD.

Gourevitch Pilip, We wish to inform you tha tomorrow we will be killed with our famies. First published 1998 by Farar, Sttaus &Giroux, New York. First published in Great Bitain 1999 by Picador.

Jaramogi Oginga Odinga, Not yet Uhuru 1967.

Gerry Caplan. Pambazuka News: Panafrican Voices for frwwdom and justice. Nairobi:2010 (issue 466).

Museveni, Yoweli. Conference in Nairobi. Nairobi:Nation News Paper. February 12th, 1990.

Kagame Alex, Inganji Kalinga, 1943, Published Kigali press LTD.

Rodney Walter How Europe Underdevelope Africa 1973. Published by Biglel-L-Ouverture publication London and Tanzania publishing house Dar-Es-Salaam.

Mohammed Babu, African Socialism 1981 published Zed press original University of Minnesota.